TACO TITAN

Taco Titan

The Glen Bell Story

By Debra Lee Baldwin

The Summit Publishing Group

The Summit Publishing Group
2000 East Lamar Blvd., Suite 600
Arlington, Texas 76006

Printed in the United States of America.

03 02 01 00 99   1 2 3 4 5

Library of Congress Cataloging-in-Publication Data

Baldwin, Debra Lee, 1952-
    Taco titan : the Glen Bell story / by Debra Lee Baldwin.
    p. cm.
  Includes index.
  ISBN 1-56530-299-0
  1. Bell, Glen William, 1923- 2. Restaurateurs--United
States--Biography. 3. Taco Bell (Firm) 4. Fast food
restaurants--United States--History. I. Title.
  TX910.5.B34 B35 1999
  338.7'6164795'092--dc21
  [B]
                              98-58150
                              CIP

Cover by KC Scott
Book Design by Creative Fuel
Index by Michael Rossa

"At one time, Glen and the McDonald brothers *were* the fast food industry. All Glen's instincts are right. His thoughts had to do with freshness, quick service and happy customers. The money didn't matter to him. The customer came first. Business people need a product, and creative types like Glen provide it."

John Galardi, founder and CEO of Wienerschnitzel restaurants

"Glen made Mexican food universal. He started something that was successful for thousands of people, and made many of them millionaires."

Carl Karcher, founder of Carl's Jr. restaurants

"Glen Bell's introduction of the taco was a coming of age, the right product at the right time. Back in the late 50s and 60s, no one thought people on the East Coast would eat tacos. They didn't understand the potential of the market."

James A. Collins, chairman of the board, Sizzler International

"In the mid-50s, I heard about a guy selling a product called 'tacos' in San Bernardino. I went up there, and Glen Bell showed me around. So I brought the fast-food taco to San Diego and put it in Jack-in-the-Box."

John Gorman, franchise consultant and former Jack-in-the-Box executive

"Glen and I grew up together. I know more about him than anyone does, and I don't know one bad thing about him. He's one of a kind, humble yet successful."

Neal Baker, founder and owner of Baker's Burgers, 30 fast-food restaurants in the San Bernardino area

"Back when I worked for Glen, he taught me to excel in speed of service, how to keep the place spotless, and how to be friendly to customers. Although we're competitors, we've stayed friends to this day."

Ed Hackbarth, founder of Del Taco, a Southern California chain of 300 fast-food restaurants

"Glen worked 18-hour days, seven days a week. When you're building a business and growing fast, it's hard. There were a lot of problems. Glen was successful because he didn't give up."

Robert L. Trujillo, real estate investor and past president of Wienerschnitzel

To Marty and Kathleen

CONTENTS

Glen Bell competes with the McDonald brothers by introducing
nineteen-cent tacos at his tiny self-serve restaurant in San Bernardino.

Glen's grandparents earn a fortune in California real estate. Their
daughter Ruth marries a charming man who can't keep a job: Glen W.
Bell Sr. Ruth struggles to feed their six children during the Depression, but pride keeps her from asking her widowed mother for help.

The Bell family moves to a ten-acre farm in the San Bernardino
Mountains. The two-room farmhouse has no electricity, telephone,
or hot water. To earn money, Glen and his siblings grow potatoes and
sell flowers door to door.

Glen lives on his own in San Bernardino while attending high school.
At age sixteen, when his money runs out, he "goes on the bum" and
rides the rails in search of work. In partnership with an eighty-three-
year-old aunt, he opens a pie business and earns money to finish school.

While in the Marine Corps, Glen serves food to top brass in Guadalcanal and learns the U.S. strategy for the Pacific front. Back in San
Bernardino, he buys an army surplus truck and hauls adobe bricks
for five cents apiece.

In his desire to create a family-oriented business, Glen leases a miniature
golf course that fails. He builds an innovative food stand that is destroyed
by a windstorm. Glen's long hours cause conflict in his first marriage.

ACKNOWLEDGMENTS

More than fifty friends, relatives, and associates of Glen W. Bell Jr. contributed to the research of his biography.

Glen's older sister, Deloris Lukens, provided details of their childhood, as did siblings Merrill Bell, Maureen Hughes, and Dorothy Cremonese as well as cousins Ed and Preston Hiefield.

Friends C. J. Busick and Rea Mowery, who, like Glen, served in the Marine Corps during World War II, gave their perspective on Guadalcanal and the Pacific front.

His lifelong friend, Neal Baker, recalled Glen's early business endeavors and those of the McDonald brothers in San Bernardino. Bernard Taylor, Glen's former father-in-law, graciously provided family data.

Glen's pre-Taco Bell business associates, who assisted his attempts to make Mexican fast food mainstream, added wisdom as well as humor. Among them are Phil Crosby, John Galardi, Ed Hackbarth, Bill Lindner, Harland Svare, and Bob Trujillo. Tod McDonald described his grandfather, Al, who with Glen formed Taco-Tia; and Ginger Toogood spoke for her deceased husband, Charley, an El Taco partner.

Bruce Burrow, Macy Coffin, Hal Ezell, Wayne Milner, Lou Novak, and Paul Wesley described Taco Bell's birth and phenomenal growth during the early sixties. Robert McKay and John Gorman told how they, as key members of Taco Bell's management team, helped Glen develop the young company's potential. Early Taco Bell investors John Kilpatrick, Lester Morris, and Bill Tilley also gave valuable insight.

Past franchisees who shared their adventures during Taco Bell's rollercoaster growth include Kermitt Bekke, Harry Buseman, Bill Cason, and Larry and Val Hahn. Present franchisees Grover Moss and Robert St. John provided practical assistance and memorabilia.

Ruth Bradley Hill, Glen's former secretary, recalled his post-Taco Bell endeavors, as did former Westside & Cherry Valley employees Frank Cimino and Gordon Ham.

Employees and associates of Bell Gardens and Bell Enterprises who helped expedite the biography include Jay Enns, David and Barbara Karle, Carole Langdon, and Gary Winkelman.

Bruce Given supplied information concerning Glen's involvement with the community of Valley Center. Susan and Michael Armstrong of Valley Center shared the poignant story of their son, Jason, which illustrates Glen's support of 4-H youth.

Andrall ("Andy") Pearson, chairman and CEO of Taco Bell's parent company, Tricon Global Restaurants, and Peter Waller, president and chief concept officer of Taco Bell, deserve special thanks for their enthusiastic support of this biography, as do Taco Bell corporate employees Ed Alfaro and Jeff Lightburn.

Literary agent James Cypher expedited the publishing process through tight deadlines.

Glen's wife Martha ("Marty") and his children Rex, Gary, and Kathleen, gave their time and memories and the encouragement that persuaded Glen to share his life story.

And Glen himself, undaunted by a task that at first seemed overwhelming, devoted a year to sifting and prioritizing photos, papers, and recollections of the past.

Debra Lee Baldwin

In the chain restaurant industry, Glen Bell stands out as one of the legendary pioneers.

When he introduced the fast-food taco during the 1950s, there was virtually no chain restaurant industry. Even McDonald's was just getting started.

In 1965, when Glen signed up his first franchisee, the concept of a Mexican fast-food restaurant chain was at best highly speculative. From that early beginning, Taco Bell has grown to become a $5 billion chain—and the dominant Mexican food purveyor in the United States.

Glen's distinctive-looking taco stands have evolved into a company that serves more than 60 million people each week and operates in sixteen countries.

In many ways, Glen epitomizes the American dream. His enormous success is the result of vision, persistence, flexibility, and, above all, a determination to serve customers better than his competitors.

Along the way, Glen was the inspiration and mentor to dozens of his franchisees—many of whom became rich by following his lead. He was a tough competitor, yet his rivals respected and admired his customer focus and integrity.

As one competitor commented, "I don't know one bad thing about Glen Bell."

As Taco Bell grew, Glen had the vision and self-confidence to stand back and delegate responsibility. This enabled his company to become national and ultimately international. His two key lieutenants, John Gorman and Robert McKay, ran the operations, while Glen provided the vision and overall direction.

Now, as part of Tricon, Taco Bell is the centerpiece of a more than $20 billion global restaurant chain. As Tricon's first chairman and CEO, I salute Glen Bell and his irreplaceable contribution to our exciting new beginning outside of PepsiCo.

The business Glen founded just thirty-five years ago stands as a monument to his towering leadership.

Andrall E. ("Andy") Pearson

Chairman and CEO, Tricon Global Restaurants, Inc.

Andy Pearson served as president of PepsiCo from 1971 to 1984. The former Harvard Business School professor expedited PepsiCo's purchase of Taco Bell in 1978 and the formation of Tricon Global Restaurants in 1997. Tricon includes Taco Bell, KFC, and Pizza Hut.

I met Glen W. Bell Jr. in the fall of 1996 when I profiled him for the *San Diego Union-Tribune.*

Glen was seventy-three, but inside him was a young man who had endured the Depression, fought in World War II, had ridden the crest of postwar prosperity after founding Taco Bell, and who had earned his first million by the age of forty-six.

With his felt cowboy hat and worn flannel jacket, Glen didn't look like a tycoon. And if tycoons are supposed to smoke cigars, drive flashy cars, and treat employees like servants, Glen didn't act like one either.

The newspaper profile led to this biography. In the living room of the ranch-style home used for Bell Gardens' offices, Glen reminisced while I made notes. But what both of us really wanted to do was to climb into his deluxe golf cart and ride around the 115-acre farm.

When we did so, we left the 1990s and returned to America's agrarian past. In many respects, Bell Gardens represents an idealized version of Glen's childhood, which was spent on small farms in Oregon and California and, as an adolescent, hitching rides aboard freight trains.

As time slowed and the present receded, Glen and I watched tractors plow neat furrows, curving them to follow the skirt of a hill. In winter, mature olive, pepper, and oak trees were green, but deciduous trees formed skeletal outlines against the sky. Rainstorms had created alluvial fans that flowed across chocolate-colored slopes.

Despite mobility hampered by Parkinson's disease, Glen piloted the golf cart with precision. Occasionally he paused to contemplate what did not yet exist, and from time to time, his thoughts surfaced to form words.

"We need something for them to look at when they come around that curve," he said. I understood that "they" were future visitors.

Fields planted with strawberries, corn, melons, and more would "show kids how things grow." Glen and his wife, Martha ("Marty"), a former schoolteacher, share a love of farming and a desire to educate and encourage young people.

At the Bell Gardens train barn one January afternoon we found three neighbors talking with Glen's railroad manager. He had been working on a quarter-scale passenger train with open-air compartments that resembled a series of loaf pans, and asked if Mr. Bell and I would care to join them for a train ride. Glen lowered himself into the caboose.

The train glided at about fifteen miles an hour through seventy-degree air and circled a lake the size of a football field. As wild ducks scooted away from the invader, their V-shaped wakes shattered the reflection of the sky. A snowy egret, white against the silver water, spread slender wings and soared to the opposite shore.

The visitors gazed at the scenery; Glen watched his guests. They pointed with outstretched arms and leaned together to talk above the rush of wind. Distant mountains were distinct through rain-washed air, their boulders gray-white against blue-green. Equestrian fences along the foothills defined ranches with horizontal white lines. When the train rattled over a trestle, the noise of rocking metal and wood was pleasantly loud, reminiscent of larger engines and bygone days.

At the end of the fifteen-minute ride, Glen asked his neighbors if they enjoyed it. One said she liked a canyon abloom with camellias; another commented on emerald fields of winter wheat; a third mentioned a miniature Victorian depot alongside the lake.

As I researched Glen's life, I spoke with many who said his goal always had been to provide pleasurable experiences for others. Glen first demonstrated this with food stands, and later with family-oriented parks. Bell's Hamburgers developed into Taco-Tia, El Taco, and finally Taco Bell. Rainbow Springs in Florida led to Westside & Cherry Valley Railway in Northern California and then to Bell Gardens.

Although Glen amassed a fortune as one of the twentieth century's most successful entrepreneurs, his life illustrates a truth that transcends monetary rewards: Accomplishment begins with vision, is fueled by commitment and determination, and is made worthwhile by the ways it benefits others.

Debra Lee Baldwin, 1998

Birth of the Fast-Food Taco
December, 1951

ON A WINDY DECEMBER MORNING IN 1951, Glen Bell arrived at his San Bernardino hamburger stand with a sign that read: "Tacos nineteen cents."

Today he recalls, "I had no idea if anyone would buy them."

As a brisk desert breeze rattled the fronds of two sixty-foot palms on the stand's east side, Glen and four employees formed patties, sliced buns, peeled potatoes, and piled hot dogs at one end of a four-foot grill.

The twenty-eight-year-old former marine could have located the refrigerator, grill, milk shake mixer, and cash register with his eyes closed. Seven days a week, Glen arrived at the 240-square-foot concrete-block building before 11 A.M. and stayed until after closing, twelve hours later.

"It was a young man's business," he recalls. "I stayed open as long as there was another customer. I had worked too hard to let even one go."

San Bernardino, sixty miles east of Los Angeles, was known for its citrus orchards, vineyards, air force base, Santa Fe Railway yards—and hamburger stands, including a popular one operated by Mac and Dick McDonald.

"I was determined to beat the competition," Glen says, "so I decided to experiment." And because Bell's Hamburgers and Hot Dogs was in a Hispanic neighborhood, "I figured if Mexican food was successful, potential competitors would write it off to my location and assume the idea wouldn't sell anywhere else. No one would copy what I was doing, and that would give me time to perfect it."

Glen's twenty-two-year-old wife, Dorothy, told him he was wasting his time: Didn't he know Mexican food had a reputation for being so spicy it burned people's mouths? It was immigrant fare, too exotic for most Americans. Besides, Spanish names were foreign and hard to pronounce.

He explained that he thought he might sell Mexican food that wasn't spicy. She replied, "Then not even Mexicans will buy it." Friends and relatives echoed his wife's opinions.

Across the street from his walk-up stand was a Mexican restaurant with a clay-tile roof and neon-outlined name. Glen recalls the fried taco: "They'd take a tortilla, soften it in fat, fold it in half, put meat in it and seal it with toothpicks. Then they'd put it in a fryer. When it came out, they'd add lettuce and cheese. It was delicious but dripped melted fat.

"I was on good terms with my neighbors and learned from them. I didn't invent the taco, but I believe I improved it. When you ordered a half dozen tacos in a restaurant, it took too long. You'd wait twenty minutes. With that method they couldn't do any volume."

In 1951, no fast-food vendors sold crisp-shelled tacos, which were uncommon on either side of the border. *Taco* means "stuffing" or "snack," and is related to the English word "tuck."

Glen envisioned a walk-up restaurant that sold tacos and other Mexican specialties as quickly as customers ordered them. He searched San Bernardino's library and bookstores for Mexican cookbooks and learned the food was too unusual to be the subject of an entire book.

Not far from his hamburger stand was a tortilla factory that scented the neighborhood with the aroma of fresh baked cornmeal. Within the *tortilleria's* warm recesses, women conversed in Spanish as they mixed a yellow dough called *masa*. Workers fed dough into a machine that stamped out thin disks, then sent the tortillas jiggling along a chain-link conveyor belt. As raw tortillas passed over jets of blue flame, they puffed into plump, round pillows. Fragrant and steaming, the tortillas collapsed as they cooled, and the women tossed them into baskets lined with clean white cloth.

Glen purchased a stack of fresh, tender tortillas and a variety of Mexican spices. Late at night, after closing, he experimented with sauces, fillings, and cooking techniques.

Instead of soft or greasy, he wanted tortillas delicately crisp and ready to be filled. "Preformed taco shells look so simple today, but back then I had to figure out a way to make them."

After weeks of experimentation, Glen developed a taco that was quick to assemble and tasty to eat. What remained to be seen was whether the new item would sell.

On the morning he intended to introduce nineteen-cent tacos, Glen heated oil in a deep fryer and inserted tortillas into a wire holder he had designed. They bubbled and hissed and emerged golden, crisp, and open about an inch. He placed a stack of ready-to-stuff shells alongside freshly made french fries beneath infrared lights and just inside a front window where customers could see them. On a stainless steel counter near a savory hamburger mixture that simmered over a low flame, he set bowls of chopped lettuce and shredded cheese.

At eleven, an employee lifted the "Closed" sign and turned it around. The first customers were Hispanic, and ordered hot dogs. Soon the grill also sizzled with hamburger patties.

San Bernardino, California, 1951. Glen (behind the order window) introduced the fast-food taco at Bell's Hamburgers, corner of Sixth and Mt. Vernon.

Glen gazed through the stand's counter-to-ceiling windows, and watched as the Santa Ana wind lifted dry leaves and sent them swirling into bushes and chain-link fences. Crows flapped their wings but made so little headway they appeared to fly in place. He looked east, located the cleft in the mountains where he had grown up, and noted that distant ridges were dusted with white, like powdered sugar.

A green car with a bullet nose, a Studebaker, pulled alongside the curb. Its driver wore a pinstriped suit, and Glen thought he might be a salesman. As the man approached the order window, the wind seemed to yank his brightly patterned tie.

Glen considered inviting him to try a taco for free. But before he made the offer, the man said, "Gimme one of those . . . " he hesitated, then squinted at the newly painted sign. ". . . take-ohs." The pitch of his voice, raised on the second syllable, made the word a question.

Glen seized a crisp folded tortilla, filled the shell one-third full of meat, sprinkled it with shredded lettuce and cheese, topped it with a spoonful of mild chili sauce, and wrapped the taco in waxed paper. In fifteen seconds the customer held it in his hand. He stood near the window, examined the taco, then bit into it.

"Juice ran down his sleeve and dripped on his tie," Glen says. "I thought, uh-oh, we're not going to be successful. We've lost this one."

The man wiped both hands on a paper napkin and dabbed his mouth. When their eyes met, Glen felt his cheeks redden. Normally he didn't stare at customers. He opened the cash register, but before he could refund nineteen cents, the man dug into his pants pocket and produced two dimes.

"That was good," he said. "Gimme another."

"Right then," Glen says, "I knew we had a winner."

Glen's Recipes for Success

#1: You build a business one customer at a time.

In the early days, I never closed when there was a customer waiting, even though I had put in twelve hours and was eager to go home. One happy customer is worth his weight in gold. He'll tell two other people about you, and those two people each will tell two others, and so on.

#2: Find the right product, then find a way to mass-produce it.

When I had my hamburger stand, similar take-out stands were springing up all over San Bernardino, and the idea was spreading to Los Angeles. If my business was going to survive and grow, I would have to apply what I knew about quick service and volume sales to a different product. It wasn't necessary to invent a new food. The challenge was to improve an existing product and find a way to mass-produce it.

#3: An innovative product will set you apart.

Imagine being handed a snack from a different culture, served in an edible container with an unusual shape. You're not sure what to expect. When you try to eat it, you hold it wrong, and the filling falls out. That's what happened with our first taco customer. Yet the crispy shell, aroma, and flavor of the "take-oh" were so good he ordered another. The fact that it was a quality product overcame the fact that it was unusual.

CHAPTER ONE

Growing Up Poor
1901-1933

A WEDDING PHOTO OF GLEN W. BELL JR.'S GRANDFATHER, taken in 1901, shows a handsome man with a trim mustache and a firm set to his jaw. Ed Johnson's eyes gaze beyond the camera. Even then he may have been thinking of California.

Maud Kirby, Ed's bride, has a serene stare and the hint of a smile. Her hair is pulled into a no-nonsense topknot, but a few curly wisps escape.

Both Ed and Maud had read *Ramona* by Helen Hunt Jackson, a romantic novel about an Irish-Indian woman. Years passed, but Ed never forgot the book's vivid Southern California setting. As snowstorms moaned outside his home, he reread descriptions of sweet oranges that ripened in January, hot desert sand, and an ocean so vast the sun set behind a distant silver line.

The Johnsons lived in Raymond, Minnesota, a farming community of white clapboard houses and tidy red barns. When Ed went to work as a rural mail carrier, he was told the job paid "sixty dollars a month, not including feed for the horses." Ed soon advanced to postmaster. He had the means to take his family west, but no way to earn a living once they arrived.

During the bitter winter of 1914, Ed saw an advertisement that described Southern California as "paradise," with ample land for all. As he scanned a list of prices, he realized there indeed was gold in California, and it was in real estate. Ed figured demand would surge after the war, and the sooner he bought land the better. He could afford several parcels.

When Ed made up his mind to move, his enthusiasm—combined with his reputation for good sense—convinced not only his wife but also relatives and friends. Relieved that many of the people she held dear in Minnesota were moving with them, Maud quickly disposed of their possessions.

Courtesy of Deloris Lukens

Ed, Maud, and their four children settled in a coastal community south of Los Angeles. Over the next few years, 1.3 million Americans also would head for the sunset. Because so many had been seduced by *Ramona*, the popular novel became required reading in California schools.

Ed invested his savings in land, and his timing was excellent. Profits from selling real estate enabled him to form an investment company in Long Beach. Ed watched new roads, homes, subdivisions, and shopping areas spread across the Los Angeles basin. At one time he owned much of the city's Signal Hill suburb, but sold it before oil was discovered beneath it. Even so, Ed did well financially and had no regrets.

Raymond, Minnesota, 1901. Glen's maternal grandparents, Maud Elvira Kirby and Ed Johnson.

Naturally, Ed and Maud were anxious to see their children well settled. They made plans to give property to one son and send the other to law school. Their daughter, Ruth, a soft-spoken beauty with dark hair and eyes, spoke of becoming a schoolteacher. At eighteen, Ruth went to Washington state to attend college near Maud's older sister, Mary, who owned a bakery. But Ruth suffered from homesickness and returned within a year.

Ruth was nineteen when she met the man who would become the father of her six children, including a son who would bear his name: Glen

William Bell. Ed and Maud urged their daughter to reconsider. There was no need for her to marry so young or so soon.

The son of an Iowa farmer, twenty-three-year-old Glen had run away from home in the eighth grade and hitchhiked to California to live with siblings. One sister's husband delivered bread from house to house in a horse-drawn wagon. A brother sold real estate. Construction labor was in demand, and Glen became a plasterer.

Ruth met Glen amid the laughter and swirl of a Long Beach amusement park. He was slender, athletic, and wore his hair combed straight back in the fashion of the time. She liked his smile and easy way of making friends. When together, she said little and blushed when he teased her.

Her parents asked Ruth if she noticed Glen's occasional errors in grammar. Ruth replied that was no way to measure a man. She would recall this years later when to annoy her, Glen deliberately used words like "*hain't*" ("isn't").

Courtesy of Maureen Hughes

They married in 1921, at the start of a decade that would be remembered for its frivolity. Women bobbed their hair, powdered newly exposed knees, and danced the Charleston in fringed skirts. Ruth experienced none of this, nor did it interest her. Like her mother, she found nothing so admirable as a clean, organized household.

Glen was pleased with his bride's adoration and with his good fortune at joining a prosperous family. The Johnsons gave the newlyweds a small lot in Lynwood, near Long Beach. Ed's first granddaughter was born in 1922. To him her name was obvious: "Ramona." Instead,

Long Beach, California, 1921. Glen's parents, Ruth Johnson Bell and Glen W. Bell Sr., on their wedding day.

Ruth and Glen chose "Deloris," a Spanish name with an Americanized spelling. Eighteen months later, on September 3, 1923, their first son was born: Glen William Bell Jr.

Long Beach, circa 1926. Glen and his older sister, Deloris.

When Deloris and Glen Jr. were four and two, Ruth experienced the first of many jarring interruptions to her household. Glen Sr.'s occasional construction jobs did not provide enough money to maintain their Lynwood home.

Deloris recalls, "As young as I was, I felt we moved from bad to worse. Both the Bell and Johnson sides of the family seemed prosperous and lived in fine homes. We moved to Euclid Court, a shabby neighborhood on an unpaved dead-end street, where ruts formed in the road when it rained. Mom was not happy, but Daddy accepted it."

Ed and Maud lavished Christmas gifts on their grandchildren, then financed the Bell family's move to a better home in Southgate, twenty miles away. According to Deloris, "Things seemed to be going well, and most importantly, Daddy was working."

A second son, Merrill—at last the Johnsons had a grandchild named after a character in *Ramona*—was born in 1927. The family's joy, however, was short-lived. Ed's heart, with its capacity for romance, generosity, and common sense, failed him. He died of a heart attack at age forty-nine. His widow was forty-seven.

Later that same year, when Glen Sr. again was unemployed and unable to support his family, Maud suggested the Bells move to Iowa, where they could live on a farm near his relatives. Glen Sr. politely refused but agreed a small farm would suit his family's needs admirably. So Maud put a down payment on a house and pasture in Oregon, where land was cheap. She hoped that crops and cattle, supplemented by her son-in-law's occasional employment, would at last make the Bells self-sufficient.

Glen Jr., five at the time, remembers how his parents loaded their belongings into a Model T Ford truck. As they traveled through the mountains, and the vehicle descended steep, unpaved roads, its brakes burned with an acrid smell. Glen Sr. pulled over, packed spare tires with stones, then attached the tires to the back with chains. As the weighted tires dragged behind the truck, they snagged bushes and rocks, raised a cloud of brown dust, and acted as supplemental brakes.

In 1929, a year after the Bells settled in southern Oregon, an event on the opposite end of the continent threatened their hopes of prosperity. A severe drop in stock market prices led to an economic crisis unprecedented in American history. Millions became unemployed, and those with jobs lived in fear of losing them.

Grocery prices were low—a loaf of bread cost ten cents—but Ruth needed at least three dollars a week to feed her family of five. When her husband could not find work, she milked the cow, made cottage cheese, and sent Deloris and Glen Jr. to sell it door-to-door for twenty cents per half-pint jar.

Ruth's older son had eyes so large and dark that neighbors commented they couldn't tell where the pupils left off and the irises began. Because politeness prevented an escape from such scrutiny, Glen Jr. would look at the floor and will his cheeks not to burn.

Ruth also made her family's clothes. Glen Jr. recalls, "One day I was walking home from school, and a girl was walking behind me. She noticed the words 'Portland Cement' bleeding out of my shirt, which Mom had made of bleached cement sacks. I couldn't have been more embarrassed."

Deloris adds, "It was a big day when there was finally enough money for a pair of shoes. And when Mom's desperately needed winter coat arrived from California, we were so happy for her."

Thanks to Ed's foresight, Maud possessed the one thing so many needed during the Depression—cash. Ruth, however, did not plead with her mother for help. To ask for money would be humiliating; to accept it, shameful.

So Maud, unaware of the Bell family's hardships, provided civilized luxuries such as private school tuition for her grandchildren. Because Maud had become a convert to Adventism, a fundamentalist Christian sect, Glen Jr. and Deloris attended a Seventh-day Adventist school. They were taught to dress modestly; study the Bible; observe the Sabbath on Saturday; and avoid drink, dancing, and other "heathen" activities.

Glen Jr. remembers his first movie: "It was *King George V* and cost fifteen cents. The Seventh-day Adventist community didn't believe in going to movies. I felt as guilty as if I'd smoked a cigarette."

Deloris also succumbed to temptation and went to see *Oliver Twist*. "Mom was in tears when she learned where I had been. We sat on the bed and cried together."

Maud also paid for violin lessons and sent the Bells a piano. During the 1920s, a piano cost about $450, enough to feed the Bell family for three years. When it arrived, Ruth's impulse was to sell it, even though her mother might think her ungrateful. But when Ruth ran her fingertips along the keys, the clear, bright music brought a flood of happy memories. Glen Sr. accompanied her on the violin, and Deloris, Glen Jr., and Merrill sang as their parents played *"The Old Spinning Wheel"* and *"My Wild Irish Rose."*

In the fall, Ruth picked and stored apples from a tree in her garden. In December, she gave them to her children as Christmas gifts. From California came toys, nuts, and candy.

Daily, as Glen Jr. and Deloris walked home from school, they saw migrants camped beneath a railroad trestle. Public schools across the nation had closed from lack of funds, and thousands of children between the ages of seven and seventeen wandered highways and stowed away on freight trains. Some were runaways, others were accompanied by their unemployed, homeless parents.

"We'd count them whenever a train went by," Glen Jr. recalls. "Sometimes there were as many as 150 on board."

Many traveled from town to town harvesting crops. In autumn, they arrived in Grants Pass to pick hops, used by local breweries to flavor ale. To earn money for schoolbooks and supplies, Deloris and Glen Jr. joined the workers.

"We camped with hordes of adults and children who slept on mats on trucks or stayed in tents," Deloris says. "At dawn, we were hustled off to long rows of vines strung up higher than we could reach." Yet "it was the most fun of the whole year." At night, in the glow of campfires, they listened to guitar music and sang camp songs.

According to Glen Jr., "We were paid by the pound, but hops don't weigh anything. They gave us gunnysacks to fill with one hundred pounds of dry, prickly flowers. I thought the owners of the hop farm must be very wealthy, but they were probably struggling like everybody else."

Relatives who visited described the Bell's small farm as "picturesque" and "lovely." Deloris remembers the flower garden her mother planted, their home's white picket fence and a "never-ending" blackberry vine.

His father, according to Glen Jr., was well liked; it's probable no friends or neighbors realized the distress he caused his wife. "My mother was kind of shy, but she was the more intelligent of the two. There was such a contrast. My dad would tell people, 'Come on over and have dinner,' and my mother would have to put on a big feed. But he didn't provide the money to pay for it, and afterward we had to get by with less."

Yet Ruth learned her greatest blessings had nothing to do with money. Late one afternoon, as Ruth read to her children, Merrill, age three, slipped away and headed for the duck pond. Glen Sr., who was milking cows, heard the boy's screams and pulled him from the water. Merrill's cold body soon stiffened and turned blue. The Bells had no phone, so Deloris and Glen Jr. ran and asked a neighbor to call the fire department. When the firemen arrived, according to a newspaper report, "there had been no signs of life in the child for more than an hour."

The rescuers placed Merrill on a table and attempted to revive him as Ruth, Deloris recalls, said "silent and mighty prayers." Ruth told God if she had her children, she needed nothing else.

"Our little wood stove got red with heat," Glen Jr. says. "They must have thought they needed lots of warm water and hot towels. I was about seven, and my face was level with the tabletop. I remember when Merrill's eyes opened."

According to the newspaper: "Merrill Bell, believed drowned for more than two hours Sunday night, was alive and well Monday . . ."

Glen Jr. adds, "Years later, when I'd get mad at him, I'd think of how we'd almost lost him."

In 1931, after a second daughter, Maureen, was born, the family moved to an Oregon community Deloris describes as "shacks, with a one-pump service station and a run-down grade school." She adds that the Bell siblings found themselves in the company of "wild, dirty children" who ate sandwiches of bread and bacon grease.

When the Great Depression entered its fourth year, and Ruth's children were ages twelve, ten, six, and two, she gave birth to her fifth child and third daughter, Dorothy. Glen Jr. says, "There wasn't enough milk to go around. Dorothy was a little baby, and the only one who got any." If there was oatmeal left from breakfast, Ruth fried it for dinner.

Oregon, circa 1932. Deloris, Merrill, and Glen wear their Sunday best, but the rickety build-ings behind them indicate hard times.

That same year, Glen Sr. qualified for the Civilian Conservation Corps (CCC), a government-funded job program. With the influx of money, the family moved to Eighth Street in Grants Pass. As a "soil soldier," he worked with crews who built roads and installed telephone lines.

While her husband was away, Ruth appointed Glen Jr., age eight, "man of the house." Deloris describes her brother as "quiet and steadfast."

Within a year, Glen Sr. quit the CCC. He complained that the work was difficult, the living conditions squalid, and the supervisors unfair. Soon the Bells were unable to pay their eight-dollars-a-month rent.

"How will we live?" Ruth demanded of her husband.

"You don't appreciate a man's efforts," Glen Sr. replied. "A wife and five children nowadays is a burden no man should bear. There's no way to sup-port them." He might "go on the bum," he told her, and join the hobos who rode the rails. She could return to California to live with her mother. The older children could go to Iowa and learn to farm with relatives. And if Maud would not take in the younger ones, Ruth's sister Edna might.

Under no circumstances, Ruth replied, would she break up her family and give her children away—in the unlikely event anyone would have them.

"I wouldn't take a million dollars for any of my children," she said, then added, "but I wouldn't give a nickel for another one." Soon afterward, Ruth wrote her mother and asked if they might come and live with her, "just until we get on our feet."

The Bells could not return to Los Angeles, Maud replied. The area, thanks to its reputation for prosperity, was overrun with thousands of migrants seeking jobs that didn't exist. Police had been posted at the state's eastern border to persuade people to turn back. Worst of all, on March 10, 1933, a major earthquake centered in Long Beach had destroyed homes and killed 120 people. Two dozen schools were seriously damaged. Streets had cracked and caved in, and people who once owned homes lived in tents. Maud's own house had been jolted off its foundation. She would be living with Edna until it could be repaired.

Yet a statement Glen Jr. had made when he was five echoed in Maud's memory: "When I grow up, I want to be a businessman like my grandpa." After weeks of anguish and prayer—combined with inquiries made through her church—Maud offered a solution she hoped would ease the Bell family's problems once and for all.

Glen's Recipes for Success

#4: There's always a way to get ahead if you're determined and creative.

People have problems today, but imagine how much worse things were during the Great Depression. My mother made our clothes from feed sacks, and we children picked flowers and sold them door-to-door. It's tempting to blame circumstances for your problems, but it's a waste of time. Instead, reach inside yourself. You'll come up with ways to cope and take pride in meeting the challenge.

#5: Family is precious!

Little children don't know the difference between riches and poverty. What mattered most to us was being able to count on our parents. We would have liked store-bought toys, nicer clothes, and better food, but those things weren't as important as feeling secure and being contributing members of a family.

#6: You create the person you become.

Growing up means taking a long, hard look at people around you and deciding which of their characteristics you want and which ones you don't. For example, my mother was resourceful and never let circumstances stand in her way. You can decide how to be, and how not to be by watching how people's actions help or hurt others.

CHAPTER TWO

Cedar Springs
1934-1936

AS RUTH READ HER MOTHER'S LETTER, it was all she could do to hold back tears of happiness.

Maud had purchased ten acres in the mountains, eighty miles east of Los Angeles and twenty miles north of San Bernardino. A half-dozen Seventh-day Adventist families, about thirty people in all, lived in Cedar Springs. Their homes dotted a valley at an elevation of 3,500 feet.

On the sloping property, Maud wrote, was a small house that Glen Sr., with his construction skills, easily could enlarge. A church, which doubled as a schoolhouse, bordered the property. The land was rocky but included a pasture and a well. Nearby was a small creek. They could have chickens, a cow or two, plant a vegetable garden, harvest apples from an old orchard, and—best of all—live rent-free. Maud offered the property as a gift to Ruth; Ed would have wanted it that way. All Maud asked was that her grandchildren regularly attend the community's church and school.

Ruth accepted. Cedar Springs sounded like heaven.

Glen Sr. spent five dollars on a 1923 White pickup truck with a long bed enclosed by high wooden sides. In the back, on top of boxes—and Ruth's piano, which lay flat—went mattresses. Above these, leaving a gap of a few feet, Glen Sr. stretched a canvas tarp, which he tied with rope on either side. To start the truck, he turned a crank in the front. Ruth and the baby sat next to him; the older children scrambled onto the mattresses in the back.

Glen Jr. recalls that the trip south, on two-lane roads, "was like lying in bed and watching the world go by."

From their sheltered vantage point, the children observed the countryside change from forest to plains. Deloris says, "It was quite an eye-opener. We had never seen cities, palm trees, or vineyards."

Outside Fresno, they followed slow trucks loaded to overflowing with fragrant bunches of grapes. Glen Jr. recalls, "They were falling off the edges of the trucks. We rigged poles and tried to reach up and grab them."

Their journey seemed over when the purple-blue San Bernardino mountains rose above the horizon. But they had not counted on difficulties presented by a high-elevation gap thirteen miles from Cedar Springs: the Cajon Pass. (Pronounced "*ka-HONE*," the word means "box" or "narrow canyon" in Spanish.) As the old truck labored up the grade in low gear, the children climbed out and walked. Drop-offs were steep, views spectacular.

As the late-summer sky deepened into night, the wind became harsh. The children, tired and chilled, talked of nothing but their new home. "But when we got to Cedar Springs, the house was just two rooms and a closet," Glen Jr. remembers. "Cold air came through cracks in the floors. I don't know how my mother stood it."

According to Deloris, "Our L-shaped, wood-frame cabin consisted of one all-purpose room, about twelve-by-twenty feet, and a ten-by-ten bedroom. Our three beds took up most of the bedroom, with just enough space to squeeze through to the closet. We kept our clothes under the beds."

How, Glen Sr. asked his wife, was he supposed to pay for lumber, bricks, and cement to fix up the house? Obviously there were no jobs in Cedar Springs. Ruth suggested he come up with a product or service he might sell in San Bernardino and neighboring communities.

In the meantime, the children eagerly explored the area. "We were in a little valley with mountains around us," Maureen says. "I loved it there. We hiked, swam in the pond, caught frogs, and trapped skunks. There were long rows of Concord grapes and manzanita bushes with red bark and

Courtesy of Maureen Hughes

Cedar Springs, California, circa 1940. Glen grew up on this ten-acre farm in the San Bernardino Mountains. During the 1960s, the valley was flooded to create Lake Silverwood.

berries that looked like little apples. The scrub oak was over our heads, and we'd hide in it. The sagebrush had a clean, refreshing smell, and in spring the fields were full of poppies and purple lupines. There was so much beauty."

Ruth's sixth and last child, John Richard, was born the next year. Glen Jr. recalls, "You can imagine how crowded it was. It was probably worse than I remember. We were all on top of each other."

He adds, "There was no electricity when we first moved there, so we had no refrigerator or electric lighting. We used kerosene lanterns. We did have cold running water because a windmill in the pasture pumped water to a five-thousand-gallon tank on the hill. The outhouse, or privy, was away from the house and hard to use at night and in cold weather. The wood cookstove was the only heat in the house. We heated water on the stove for baths and washing dishes."

Maureen says, "We used to take baths in the kitchen, Dorothy and I together. Our mother heated water in a huge copper pot that took up two burners, then poured it into a big galvanized tub on the floor. The dirtiest members of the family used the bath water last. In summer, we took a bar of soap and went to the crik (creek). We took our baths on Friday, because church was Saturday."

Deloris helped her mother clean house each Friday. "It had to be finished that evening for the beginning of the Sabbath. The piano and other furniture were polished to a shine and our clothes laid out for Sabbath School."

Ruth, however, stayed home while her children attended church. According to Deloris, "She was a religious person, but if she couldn't go well dressed, she didn't go." Ruth also felt embarrassed "at our poor living conditions whenever relatives visited."

Courtesy of Maureen Hughes

Cedar Springs, circa 1936. Ruth Bell poses with her children in front of the 1923 White truck that brought the Bells back to California. Left to right: Glen Jr. (seated on truck); Deloris holding Dorothy; Ruth and Merrill; Maureen (seated on fender); visiting cousin, Kenny Worrell.

Their cousin, Ed Hiefield, one of Ruth's sister Edna's two sons, finds this surprising. "Our family went to the mountains two or three times a year. Aunt Ruth was a great cook. She was really something—a nice, easy-going person. I can truthfully say neither my mother nor my uncles ever said a word about poverty. The feeling the rest of the family had for Ruth was admiration."

Such visits were planned by mail. Glen Jr. recalls, "There were no telephones in Cedar Springs. I shied away from telephones anyway. I was always self-conscious, and until I was thirteen or fourteen, I never used one."

In the summer the children earned money by picking strawberries on a neighboring farm. Glen Jr. also grew and harvested potatoes and sold them for a penny a pound, one dollar for a hundred-pound bag. "I used the money to buy a bicycle. It cost twenty-five dollars. The down payment was five dollars."

Occasionally Glen Sr. would raise and sell calves, which he transported in the back of their car.

"I was embarrassed by our car," Glen Jr. says. "It was a 1929 Packard, and there was cardboard where a side window used to be."

In the winter, the Bell children picked and sold mistletoe and slid down slopes cushioned with snow. The one-room schoolhouse smelled of wood smoke and soup that students brought for lunch and heated on the cast-iron stove.

Most girls wore long stockings; the Bell girls did not. Nor did they own store-bought clothes. According to Maureen, "Back then, chicken feed came in cloth sacks, and our mother washed them and made blouses. We liked them. They had pretty floral prints."

Glen Jr. adds, "Shoes were expensive, and we outgrew them fast. I ordered some boots from the Sears catalog. They looked like they'd take rough wear because they had thick soles. When they came, they felt good but had a big squeak. It drove me nuts in class. I tried soaking them in water. Nothing helped, but I wore them anyway. I'd paid three dollars for them, which was a good day's wages."

Their parents agreed the addition of a large living room was a priority. Glen Jr. says, "My mother thought my father should do the things we needed first, but instead of walls he built a fireplace, then the floor. I used to dream of the day a lumber truck would come up the driveway, and how the room would look." Glen Sr. finished the room in 1940, five years after they arrived in Cedar Springs.

As weather allowed, the older children slept outside the front door in the unfinished room, or under the canopy of nearby oaks. Glen Jr. recalls, "Whenever anyone came to visit, they walked through our bedroom." The children heard the occasional eerie yowl of a bobcat, but few wild animals were hostile. "There were mostly deer and rabbits. The neighbor's bull scared us more than anything."

Despite health threats that ranged from poison oak to rock slides, the Bell children seldom needed medical attention. In any case, "Doctors were out of the question," says Deloris. When Maureen suffered a head injury, she was taken to a hospital in San Bernardino, an hour's drive away.

Deloris' arm swelled after a bicycle accident. "I couldn't bend it. It finally healed after many saltwater baths."

When Ruth and her daughters visited Mrs. Westfall, a neighbor, they covered their noses and mouths with handkerchiefs. "We stood a foot away from her bed," Deloris says. "She was dying of tuberculosis."

Glen Sr. found intermittent work doing plastering for neighbors. "He did a better job for them than he did for us," Glen Jr. recalls. "He used cardboard in our house, instead of plasterboard, and the walls were wavy."

Always on the lookout for a bargain, their father bought hundreds of pounds of gladiolus bulbs for a dollar, with the intent of selling the flowers when they bloomed. The following autumn, Deloris and Glen Jr. helped him clear a field and plant the bulbs. That winter Glen Sr., who "shopped" at dumps, collected square tin containers to hold the cut flowers he planned to sell. In spring, Deloris recalls, "the flowers were beautiful beyond all expectations, deep red and yellow and white."

According to Glen Jr., "We sold bouquets door-to-door in mountain resorts and down below. I kind of balked at it. The younger ones did better because they were cute." In San Bernardino, he found a barber willing to trade a haircut for a bouquet, saving them twenty-five cents each.

During monthly trips to town, the Bells bought gasoline for fifteen cents a gallon, kerosene, chicken feed, hay, flour, hamburger, oatmeal, sugar, soap, seeds to start crops, and produce they couldn't grow at home. Citrus groves encircled San Bernardino like a green wreath, and a dozen oranges cost a penny.

"We were pretty much self-sufficient in the mountains," Glen Jr. recalls. "We had milk, eggs, and chicken plus vegetables and apples in season. We never went hungry, but we had a limited diet." Occasionally, they visited a factory that made puffed wheat and rice. "We'd buy seconds, a few bags each. It had more chaff, but it was a treat. We really got tired of oatmeal."

On the way home, they stopped at a bakery. "We'd be there at 6 P.M., and the lady selling bread would see us standing outside in the back. We must have looked hungry. They sold day-old bread in barrels for seventy-five cents. She'd take each loaf and break it in half so it couldn't be resold. We just hoped there'd be doughnuts or cinnamon rolls."

To prevent the bread from becoming moldy, Ruth dried it. She placed chunks in flour sacks and hung them from the rafters. "A big part of our diet was bread pudding, bread-and-gravy, and toast," Glen Jr. remembers. "I still like bread in a bowl with milk poured over it."

Like his mother, Glen Jr. enjoyed cooking. Maureen recalls that the french fries he made when babysitting "were so thin, and so good."

In 1935, the Roosevelt administration implemented a massive federally funded job program. Glen Sr. temporarily left Cedar Springs to join 8.5 million Americans who built WPA (Works Progress Administration) bridges, airports, public parks, and highways. Salaries averaged $41.57 a month. According to Glen Jr., "My dad earned $30 a month. He mailed home $27 and kept $3 for his shaving gear."

Courtesy of Dorothy Cremonese

Cedar Springs, circa 1938. Ruth Bell.

Glen Jr. adds, "The Depression was the sort of thing you never forget. It wasn't over until the war started. I don't like to say the war was a good thing, but in that sense it was. People have a hard time understanding the thinking in those days. For example, when spring rains flooded San Bernardino, I looked across the river where it flowed over the highway and saw cars and fire trucks stranded in the water. It was a disaster, but somehow it gave me a good feeling. Fixing the damage would help create jobs."

In 1936, at age fourteen, Deloris left Cedar Springs to live with Maud and attend a private Seventh-day Adventist academy in Arlington, twenty miles south of San Bernardino. "I knew from observing visitors from down below that my wardrobe would never do," she says.

Fortunately, Maud provided money for school clothes. Deloris looked forward to buying fashionable—and flattering—skirts and blouses, but to her dismay, her parents took her to Mode-O-Day in San Bernardino, a store that catered to housewives. Even so, Deloris recalls that the cotton-print dresses, which had to be shortened, "were the best part of my wardrobe."

Glen Jr. would turn fourteen in September 1937, and was determined to go to high school, even though the closest one was in San Bernardino. He could commute on foot and by bus, but the trip would take three hours each way—longer if the weather was bad. Another option was to live in San Bernardino. For a dollar a day, he could board with a family in town.

"If I boarded-out five days a week and went home on weekends, I needed a minimum of twenty dollars a month." Of course, his parents did not have the money, and Ruth was too proud to ask Maud. Glen Jr. could leave Cedar Springs before dawn and return home after dark—or he could find a way, on his own, to pay twenty dollars a month.

Glen's Recipes for Success

#7: Learn to enjoy nature's free and abundant beauty.

Most people today would feel sorry for a family of eight living in a two-room mountain cabin without a TV. Certainly, it was hard on my mother. But we children discovered the entertainment value of rocky creeks, hiking trails, and trees to climb. Thanks to growing up in Cedar Springs, I still value the natural beauty of trees and raw land.

#8: Don't be embarrassed by your circumstances if you're working hard to improve them.

My mother was sensitive about our poor living conditions and didn't realize that neighbors and visitors admired her good nature, hard work, and hospitality. She might have been a lot happier if she hadn't assumed others felt sorry for her.

#9: Always be on the lookout for a bargain.

When every penny is precious, you realize how important it is to save money and spend it wisely. You're careful not to waste anything. Pretty soon thrift becomes a virtue, and you take pride in practicing it. Later, even though you can afford luxuries, you take care of the things you have, and you appreciate getting a good deal.

CHAPTER THREE

Hobo Adventures
1937-1941

FEW SOUNDS DISTURBED THE SILENCE OF CEDAR SPRINGS, and those that did were too routine for residents to notice. Creeks murmured after spring rains; mockingbirds mimicked the chatter of mountain jays; and freight trains, nine miles distant, chugged up the steep grade to Summit.

To fourteen-year-old Glen Bell, a freight train represented excitement and adventure. To his father, it was free transportation. Despite the risk—deaths and injuries to riders who jumped aboard moving trains numbered in the hundreds every year—Glen's father showed him how it was done.

"There's a steel ladder on boxcars," Glen says. "Generally, you grab the ladder and climb onto the top of a boxcar. I don't recommend anyone try it. When you're running alongside a train, watching the place where you want to grab on, you can trip on a board or step in a hole. If you don't get a good hold, you can lose a leg or an arm."

With Deloris gone to live with Maud, Glen became the oldest of five children. When the family sat down to dinner, there never seemed to be enough food, and he waited until the others filled their plates. Perhaps it was time for him to leave, too.

A sound he had taken for granted, and indeed had ceased to hear, became an incessant invitation. On warm summer evenings, after his

Sawpit Canyon, circa 1940. Glen and his siblings explored the San Bernardino Mountains near Cedar Springs. His childhood adventures gave Glen a lifelong love of wooded terrain, rocky creeks, and waterfalls.

chores were done, Glen hiked to the top of the mountain where trains switched engines. More often than not, he succumbed to temptation and climbed aboard. The ride down the Cajon Pass was exhilarating. As the train rushed toward a curve, its brakes shrieked, and metal against metal created showers of sparks. "It was really something to see at night, whether you were looking down from the top of a boxcar or standing alongside the tracks."

From Barstow, seventy-six miles east of San Bernardino, trains snaked through the desert to Las Vegas at eighty to ninety miles an hour. "You also could go northwest to Bakersfield through Tehachapi, through tunnel after tunnel," Glen says. "Tunnels were loud and exciting, but there was a lot of black smoke. We couldn't breathe too well and were glad to get out."

Despite railroad "bulls" (police) paid to prevent railway hitchhikers, hobos routinely rode within, underneath, on top of, and clinging to the sides of boxcars. Glen found hobos to be, for the most part, clean, respectable, and courteous. They advised him to watch for flatcars loaded with automobiles. "If you found a car that was unlocked, you'd get a deluxe ride."

Such excursions assuaged his restlessness, but by the end of the summer of 1937, Glen had outgrown Cedar Springs. Apart from family, the tiny mountain community had little to offer him. His goal was to attend high school down below, and he was willing to work to pay for room and board. But an hour's unskilled labor—if he was lucky enough to find a job—paid only twenty-five cents.

Glen explained his circumstances to school district officials and learned that students who lived in outlying areas, too far to commute daily, were allotted fourteen dollars a month. He also qualified for assistance from the National Youth Administration (NYA), a government-funded work program. The NYA would pay Glen six dollars a month to clean blackboards after school.

But twenty dollars a month was the minimum he needed. To pay for necessities such as books, school supplies, clothes, shoes, and haircuts, he made deliveries for a dairy. "It was so early that customers didn't come to the door. Usually I put the milk in an icebox on the back porch."

A visit to the dentist cost him two dollars. "A really good dentist was three dollars," he recalls. Luxuries such as candy bars were a nickel apiece, as were streetcar rides downtown. For less than a dollar, Glen could have ridden the red car south to Arlington, near Riverside, to visit his grandmother and older sister. Instead he rode his bicycle for the forty-mile round-trip.

"Deloris was lucky to be able to live with someone in her own family," Glen says. "During the Depression, people would rent a big old house, then rent out rooms. It helped everyone live a little better." But taking in boarders also was a sign of desperation in tough times, and hosts were sensitive about it. "Sometimes when they had company, they'd pretend they were helping us, instead of doing it for the money. It was embarrassing for us boarders."

Glen continues, "Each of the places I stayed was a little different. The first was a typical boarding house with a big dining room table. We all came together for dinner. The boys would go out later. No one supervised us." He also lived at the YMCA for three dollars a week, but had to buy his own food. "There was a chicken pie place across the street—fifteen cents with coleslaw."

Occasionally a host was eccentric. The head of one family, a devotee of one of many health fads popular during the thirties, insisted that Glen drink a ten-ounce glass of warm water every morning. Others offered unexpected extras. Glen lived with a couple who let him come in late and fix himself a snack. Later he boarded with a family who had, to his shy delight, three teenage daughters.

Hosts also expected youthful boarders to behave like sedate adults. "We'd go outside and play football after dinner," Glen recalls. "One evening, the man of the house came out and said, 'I can't have these boys on the front lawn.' A lady across the street heard him and said, 'Those boys can play on *my* lawn any time they want.' That made us feel good."

The woman across the street, Mrs. Johnson, was the wife of the barber who had given Glen a haircut in exchange for a bouquet. Glen remembers her as "a real good person. She'd say, 'You can come any time, but I'm not going to feed you.' Then she'd make a big batch of biscuits."

When her husband came home from work, they'd sit at a table and stack and restack the quarters he'd earned. "They sort of played with them. It amounted to three dollars on a slow day and maybe six dollars on a Saturday." Mr. Johnson also preached the virtues of thrift. "When he rinsed out a milk bottle, he'd drink the water mixed with milk and tell me, 'Don't throw anything away.'"

Their son Del, born when Mrs. Johnson was in her forties, was Glen's age, but was rarely home. "He'd paid four dollars for a Model T Ford," Glen recalls. "It was just a frame and engine. It would break down in the middle of a busy intersection, and Del and his friends would swarm all over it to get it going again."

Glen returned to Cedar Springs on Fridays, at the end of the school week. When it rained, he rode the school bus, which averaged ten miles an hour, instead of a freight train, which labored up the mountain at fifteen to twenty miles an hour.

"The kids on the Crestline bus were wild and ornery," Glen recalls. "I felt sorry for the driver. He'd drop the flat wooden arm that signaled a turn, then forget about it, and cars would honk at the bus. Of course, the kids made the most of that. Those old buses were hard to shift. Sometimes he'd have to come to a stop to match up the gears. We did a slow crawl up the Cajon Pass."

By the summer of his sixteenth year, Glen was six feet tall, weighed 160 pounds, and had toned his muscles in high school boxing matches. If he maintained his grade point average, he would qualify for college after graduation. To earn money for his senior year, Glen raised veal calves, harvested and sold potatoes and gladiolus bulbs, and chopped wood for Cedar Springs neighbors. Ruth also put him to work.

"I'd be down with the mule in the field, and my mother would call me whenever one of the better radio shows would come on. At 6 P.M. Bob Hope would be on, then 6:30 would be Fibber McGee and Molly, then the Hit Parade of popular tunes, or Jack Benny." Maud had given the Bells a battery-operated Philco radio, which filled a wooden cabinet three feet tall and two feet wide.

With money he earned, Glen bought a Model A Ford for twenty-seven dollars. But "it was my downfall."

At times the ten-year-old sedan seemed ready to shake apart. "It wasn't a heavy car," Glen recalls. "It had hard tires and springs instead of shocks. It really jerked around, going over potholes. And on the way from San Bernardino to Cedar Springs, it would overheat." The car's tire patch kit came in handy on rutted, rock-strewn mountain roads. "Pulling the tire off the rim was a pretty tough job. Even so, taking apart a Model A was easier than riding in one."

Deloris, who by then attended nursing school in Los Angeles, remembers a visit from her brother: "He let me drive his Model A down Alameda Boulevard for a few blocks, but I barely missed a semi truck, and a policeman warned me to drive more carefully. Glen also gave me three dollars so I could buy some things I needed. It was a lot of money to me at the time, and probably to him as well."

Glen treated Mr. and Mrs. Johnson to a few outings. "It was a big deal to them," he says. And when his younger siblings and their friends begged for a ride, "We'd pack four kids in the front and two in the rumble seat." If they stopped for ten-cent hamburgers and drinks, Glen invariably paid. "A man and his wife had a little metal hamburger cart near the high school," Glen recalls. "The grill was so close you could almost reach over and turn your own hamburger. When they put onions on the grill and fried them, it smelled really good and attracted customers."

Glen's brother Merrill adds, "Glen used to say, when people were about broke with very little money, they would spend their last dime on a hamburger."

Yet by summer's end, Glen had no dimes left. "I couldn't own a car and stretch out my money. It was too expensive to operate, and it left me in bad financial shape." He sold the car by Christmas, but "I owed what I got for it. Once you get behind, it's tough. I didn't have enough to pay the people I wanted to board with. I was clean broke." He left San Bernardino and returned to the mountains.

If Ruth felt concern when Glen told her he planned to ride the rails in search of a job, she didn't show it. Her oldest son had lived on his own for two years and was, for all practical purposes, independent. She also knew how much he wanted to finish school. Glen asked his high school best friend, Neal Baker, to "go on the bum" with him.

"I told him, not on your life," Neal says. "Glen's always been kind of a daredevil, but he could take care of himself."

In mid-January, Glen hiked to Summit and boarded an empty flatcar. "It was cold and windy, but at sixteen you can take a lot." Winter was the worst time to ride the rails. Hobos told of riders who had slipped from rain-slick ladders. Others had frozen to death while traveling through high mountain passes.

There were no jobs in Victorville or Barstow. "You can't help thinking, maybe there's something down the line," Glen says. At Boulder Dam, just past Las Vegas, he found no work but made friends with a boy his age. Glen shared with him the remainder of the food he had brought from home. When they separated, the boy told him, "If you're ever in Indianapolis, look me up."

At each city he passed through, Glen asked restaurant owners to let him wash dishes or mop floors in exchange for a meal. "I could pay my way, but I couldn't get ahead. It didn't take long until I had the feeling of the homeless. It's funny how you can get that down feeling, like you're not worth anything."

In residential neighborhoods, he went door-to-door, asked for work, and endured refusals. Hobos explained to him the meaning of symbols they sketched on fence posts. For example, the letter "T" drawn at an angle meant "Trouble—get out of here fast!" They also advised him not to accept an invitation to eat inside. A gentleman hobo always asked a housewife to "hand out" his food.

Glen looked for hobo campgrounds, or "jungles," on the outskirts of populated areas near water and shelter. A riverbed beneath a trestle was ideal, especially if nearby trees provided firewood and a place to hang wash.

"You might contribute some food from the back of a grocery store, like a crib of wilted lettuce," Glen says. "Hobos would share with anybody. There was a camaraderie. We all had something in common; we were people who were capable of work, but there was no work available."

A typical hobo "mulligan stew" was a mix of meat and vegetables, flavored with onions, bacon, and cayenne pepper. After supper, they cleaned their pots and pans and hung them from tree branches. Late into the night, as campfires crackled, hobos recited poetry, told stories, sang songs, and discussed the perils and advantages of various railroad stops. They warned Glen the bulls at his next destination, Salt Lake City, would give him a brutal beating if they caught him.

Glen left for Salt Lake at dusk to avoid detection and, from the top of a boxcar, scanned the horizon. At last the lights of the city glittered with brittle clarity. "I jumped off when I thought I was a mile or two out of town, but I misjudged it," Glen says. "I had to walk twenty miles. The night was cold, and I didn't have proper clothing."

After daybreak, he went to "Sally," the Salvation Army, and received a free overcoat. He bought a penny postcard, wrote to his mother, assured her of his safety, and asked her to mail his December NYA check to General Delivery, Indianapolis. As he waited alongside the tracks on the outskirts of Salt Lake City, an off-duty policeman in a patrol car advised him, "You'll have a hard time getting a ride east; the trains are so far apart." He offered Glen a ride downtown, showed him the Temple and Tabernacle, then suggested a warm place to stay: the jail. "I checked my wallet like the 'regular customers' and got a good night's sleep."

By the time he arrived at the home of the boy he had met at Boulder Dam, Glen was as dirty and unshaven as any bum. "I didn't get a wide-open invitation to stay overnight," he recalls. He left without asking for food, water, or a place to sleep.

To cash the six-dollar NYA check, "I went to a bank with a sidewalk window. A girl spoke through a microphone, and everyone on the sidewalk heard her say, 'We don't cash out-of-town checks.' I was really embarrassed." But the bank's manager helped him, and Glen spent fifteen cents on a movie, which he sat through twice because the theater was warm. Before he left Indianapolis, he paid "two bits" (twenty-five cents) for a bed and bath at the YMCA.

From Indianapolis he rode the rails to Alexander, Iowa, where his father's cousins, the Larsens, owned a farm. "I had never met them, and I don't know what they thought of me. There weren't many occasions when boys came back to Iowa from California."

Glen's middle name, William, honored his grandfather and family patriarch, William Bell, who had been a community leader in Alexander before his death in 1921 at age sixty-three. William built a spacious home and owned a large farm, cattle ranch, and downtown drug store. Four of his six children had moved west to California.

The Depression had been hard on the Larsens, but they raised their own food and ate heartily. Glen says, "I've never seen such plates of food. For breakfast each boy ate a half dozen eggs and a huge helping of fried potatoes. They needed it because they worked hard." In early spring, Glen drove a tractor and disked corn into the ground. "The cab wasn't enclosed, and you couldn't wear enough clothes to keep warm."

After the new crop had been seeded, Glen hitchhiked home. His four-month absence had spared his mother the burden of another mouth to feed, yet he had earned no money for school.

A Cedar Springs neighbor, Mrs. Reynolds, asked Glen to escort her and her two daughters to Washington state, where her husband had found work. Ruth urged her son to go; a much-loved aunt lived in Tacoma. Glen drove the Reynolds' Model A "straight through" and briefly fell in love with one of the daughters.

At eighty-three, Glen's great-aunt Mary Dye was twenty-four years older than her sister, Maud, and in better health. Soft-spoken and sweet-natured, Aunt Mary had informally adopted, in her words, "so many children I've lost count." Family records indicate the number to be about sixty, including several wayward teenage girls and a baby left on her doorstep. Like Maud, Aunt Mary was a devout Seventh-day Adventist.

"Every Saturday, she got into her 1930 Chevrolet and drove straight to church and straight home," Glen says. "I was just dying to drive her car, but she never gave me the chance."

Aunt Mary lived alone in a faded two-story Victorian farmhouse on property that occupied a square block. Included was a garden, a barn with a milk cow, and a small bakery she had operated to earn money after her husband died. The business had become too much for her, and its equipment sat idle.

Despite the temptations of summer and a new city to explore, Glen spent hours in the unused kitchen. As he opened the doors of large ovens and examined racks and dials, Aunt Mary explained how she had used various beaters, bowls, and cooking implements. He tried to imagine the customers and asked which baked goods they liked best.

June was blackberry season, and Glen begged Aunt Mary to show him how to make a pie. He recalls, "At that time, small fruit pies about the size of your hand cost five cents apiece in grocery stores. But they were made of canned fruit with lots of cornstarch." Aunt Mary's pie, with its flaky crust and fresh filling, was clearly superior. When he learned the bakery was capable of producing three hundred to four hundred six-inch pies a day, Glen realized he'd finally found a way to earn money despite the Depression.

He and Aunt Mary named their venture "Mrs. Dye's Homemade Pies." Aunt Mary picked berries; Glen rolled out piecrusts. "I got really fast at it. I learned, with pie dough, the less you mix it, the more tender it is."

He started every morning at 5 A.M. As mist from the lake glowed red-orange then lightened to yellow-white, Mrs. Dye's bakery exuded the buttery scent of hot piecrust and the tangy perfume of fresh-cooked berries. Glen baked twenty to thirty pies at a time. When they cooled, he slid them out of their tins and into paper bags.

At 10 A.M., two salesmen he had hired arrived. "They were grown men. In those days everyone needed a job, and we kept them busy." They packed the pies two-deep in shallow boxes, sold them door-to-door for ten cents each, and received a cash commission.

The bakery also had a machine that made puffed rice and puffed wheat. Glen recalls, "Like it used to say in cereal ads, it was 'shot out of a cannon.' The barrel was twelve inches in diameter and six feet long. You'd load the head with whole-grain wheat or rice, and when it heated through, it would explode all at once like popcorn." The electric cannon propelled warm puffed grains into a wire cage four feet deep. The chaff fell through the wire.

After berry season, Glen persuaded Aunt Mary to sell bags of puffed wheat and rice; to let him make pies from canned apples purchased from a wholesaler; and to make "snowballs—cake in the middle, marshmallow dipped in coconut on the outside, five cents apiece."

At summer's end, Glen and Aunt Mary split three thousand dollars profit. "We did so well, I probably wouldn't have returned to San Bernardino if I hadn't been homesick and wanted to graduate from San Bernardino High. Also, I'd met my goal, and I figured the business wouldn't do as well in wintertime. It was a great experience. I learned a lot, and it gave me confidence. It also gave me a dream. I imagined some day I might have a little food stand."

That same summer, back in San Bernardino, two brothers pursued a similar dream when they opened a drive-in on busy E Street. Customers

Glen's senior class photo. He graduated from San Bernardino High School in 1941.

sat in their cars, and waitresses called "carhops" took orders and delivered food on hook-on trays. Although Mac and Dick McDonald's twenty-five-item menu included barbecued ribs and pork sandwiches, served on china plates with silverware, Glen—as he completed his final year of high school—preferred savory onion-scented hamburgers from the metal cart down the street.

Glen's Recipes for Success

#10: When you overextend yourself financially, it's twice as hard to get ahead.

When I was sixteen, I bought a car with money I earned, but I didn't give much thought to how I was going to pay for its upkeep. Sure enough, it was too expensive, and it used up the money I needed for school. Not planning ahead almost cost me a high school diploma.

#11: A group is made up of individuals.

During the Depression, hobos were the equivalent of homeless people today. As I got to know them, I saw how each one was different. Some were clever and tough. Others were sentimental and funny. A few were dangerous and untrustworthy. Whatever generalizations I had about hobos as a group disappeared when they became individuals with names and faces.

#12: Work that makes you lose track of time will bring out the best in you.

After Aunt Mary showed me around her bakery, I could hardly sleep at night because I was thinking about its potential. I could see myself using her equipment, making a good product, and selling it to customers. I got so caught up in the idea, I didn't care about anything else. It's true that all I did that summer was work, but it also was the most fun I'd ever had.

CHAPTER FOUR

World War II
1942-1946

ON DECEMBER 7, 1941, AT 11 A.M., eighteen-year-old Glen Bell and
two other employees of a Summit Valley cattle ranch bumped along a dirt
lane in a pickup truck. The radio buzzed, then hummed with an "important announcement" that made the startled driver slam on the brakes. As
wind sighed through a golden meadow of wild oats, and dust raised by the
truck tires settled, the young men absorbed news of a distant locale with an
exotic name: Pearl Harbor.

When America went to war, jobs at last were plentiful. Glen's father not
only became employed at a shipyard in Long Beach, he was told he couldn't
quit "for the duration." The Bell family moved temporarily to a small
house in the Compton area of Los Angeles.

"It was the first time my mother got the satisfaction of a regular paycheck," Glen says. "War housing wasn't much, but it was better than what
she had become accustomed to."

In the summer of 1942, Glen filled in for U.S. Forestry Service workers
gone to war. The lonely job entailed long vigils in a lookout tower at
the top of a mountain near Cedar Springs. "The Depression was not
yet over, and I watched people cross the Cajon Pass, on their way west,
with mattresses strapped to the top of their cars. At night I could see
their campfires."

"We had no phone contact with Glen," Deloris recalls. "Mom insisted, and I happily agreed to drive us both to visit him. It turned out to be a long trip on a dangerous dirt road." At the isolated location, as wind whipped their skirts, the two women climbed a narrow, two-story ladder to the tower. They found Glen seriously ill with the mumps. "We took him home, eighty miles to Compton, to recover."

Courtesy of Deloris Lukens

A photo of Deloris, age twenty, in a tailored Navy uniform, shows a pretty girl with sparkling eyes, pertly curled hair, and a smile that might have launched a thousand ships. When Deloris joined the war effort, she reluctantly left her grandmother. "I had been her caretaker on a third-shift basis at Seventh-day Adventist sanitariums." Maud suffered from Parkinson's disease, a neurologic disorder that causes muscle tremors, a rigid posture, and slowness of motion.

In the fall of 1942, Glen worked as a carpenter at the marine base in Barstow. "The temperature was 115 degrees on the roof of the airplane hangars," he recalls.

Glen's older sister Deloris served in the navy during World War II.

In January 1943, he joined the marines. "I was at the Marine Corps recruit depot in San Diego six weeks, then two weeks at Camp Eliot, and then we shipped out." He had two liberties before he left, but travel was difficult. "There were few buses. The train station was like a cattle stampede."

Yet Glen managed a last visit to his family. His sisters, Dorothy, nine, and Maureen, eleven, fingered the stiff wool of his new uniform and begged to try on his hat. "My mother was one to hold in her emotions," Glen says. Yet when Ruth said goodbye to him, "she broke down and cried."

With its sons and daughters away at war, the nation pulsed with patriotism. Ruth donated aluminum pots and pans to be made into munitions. She planted a "victory garden" because, according to *Life* magazine, "commercial farmers are busy feeding the army." After reading a butcher shop sign with a drawing of a hand grenade

Long Beach, 1943. Glen paid a brief visit to his family before going to war. Left to right: Maureen, Merrill, John Richard, Glen, Dorothy (in front of their mother, Ruth), and Glen Bell Sr.

("Housewives! Save waste fats for explosives!"), Ruth funneled bacon grease into tin cans.

When star-emblazoned signs on street corners advised: "The national defense needs waste paper! Save it! Sell it!" the Bell household became cluttered with stacks of newspaper and cardboard. Maureen and Dorothy accumulated used toothpaste tubes; their father donated old rubber tires. Despite at last being able to afford them, Ruth did without nylon stockings. The navy needed them to make gunpowder bags.

To Ruth's dismay, Merrill, fifteen, expressed an eagerness to go to war. Young men who were not in uniform were subject to public contempt.

Glen's life-long best friend, Neal Baker, says, "I'm blind in my right eye, so I couldn't be drafted. I felt guilty, because all my friends went off to war. I figured at least I could help out, so I got a job at the Quartermaster Depot warehouse. I distributed food to training camps and worked as a checker on the docks. But I looked healthy, and people made unkind comments."

Glen had no idea where the *USS Rochambeau*, a former French cruise ship, was headed. "Nothing prepares you for the experience of sleeping in a room with sixty men packed into bunks fourteen inches apart, stacked six high. There were no mattresses, just stretched canvas stitched on each side with rope. If a guy's bunk sags, you have to hold your stomach in. We had to string a rifle down one side, and your gas mask was right there.

"We'd hit one good wave, and I'd get sicker by the minute. One night I slung a hammock between two trucks on the top deck, and the ship started rolling so much I thought I was going to swing overboard. Then a sudden thunderstorm came up and soaked us."

Much of the day was spent in the "chow line." Troops ate standing. "Tables were chest-high and had raised edges so the trays wouldn't slide off. But every now and then, in rough seas, all the food would fall onto the floor."

After fourteen days, Glen landed in Noumea, New Caledonia, where he worked for several weeks as a waiter in the First Marine Amphibious Corps officers' mess. As luck would have it, a general's aide assigned to scout waiters to serve high-level brass noticed him. Though unskilled at food service, Glen demonstrated qualities the aide deemed essential: The nineteen-year-old was polite, deferential, eager to please, and—most importantly—disinclined to talk.

Glen was sent to Guadalcanal shortly after U.S. forces, led by Maj. Gen. Alexander Vandegrift (commanding general of the First Marine Amphibious Corps), wrested the equatorial island from the Japanese. During six months of fighting, with a loss of fifteen hundred American lives and twenty-five thousand Japanese killed or wounded, a rutted airstrip built by the enemy was claimed, then renamed Henderson Field. During mopping-up operations, soldiers continued to scour the island's near-impenetrable jungle for the enemy.

Newcomers to Guadalcanal anticipated a tropical paradise. Instead, they found a hostile jungle populated with shrill birds and unknown reptiles.

"It was humid, hot, sticky, and buggy," Glen recalls. Beneath towering coconut palms grew razor-sharp *kunai* grass. Jeeps splattered black mud that reeked of rotting vegetation. Every afternoon, white clouds boiled above the island's eight-thousand-foot peaks, then soaked the camp with thick thunderstorms. At night, the throbbing of frogs joined the jungle's endless, eerie rhythms.

Glen's marine enlistment photo, 1943 (age nineteen). During World War II, Glen had the remarkable good fortune to serve food to generals and other top brass and to overhear their battle strategies.

Letters brought welcome memories of home. Mrs. Johnson, back in San Bernardino, wrote to thank Glen for remodeling their garage into a studio apartment before he left, and told him the rent provided a much-needed supplement to their income.

"She also opened her home to servicemen who needed a place to stay," Glen says. "Even if all she had to offer was the living room sofa, she never said no."

Mrs. Johnson mentioned her son was stationed in France, so Glen sent Del Johnson a letter. "I joked about how easy he must have it in Europe and how lucky he was to be there compared to where we were. He was a fun-loving guy, a good-looking kid. He married young, just before the war started." Months later, Glen's letter to Del returned, unopened. Stamped on the outside was the word "Deceased."

His natural shyness landed Glen a two-year job on Guadalcanal that he describes as "the very best one for a PFC (Private First Class). I couldn't have thought of anything better, if you have to be over there."

For the first few months, Glen served breakfast, lunch, and dinner to Vandegrift, whose Guadalcanal strategy earned him appointment to Marine Corps Commandant; and later (after Vandegrift returned to the States) to Brig. Gen. Roy Stanley Geiger, a naval aviator and commander of Marine Air Wing One—in addition to other high-ranking officers. Visitors included Vice Admiral William "Bull" Halsey, who replaced Vice Admiral Robert Ghormley as commander of the Pacific theater; Rear Admiral T. S. Wilkinson; and American journalist H. V. Kaltenborn.

"At first, I had a hard time keeping track of the admirals and generals," Glen says. "I had to serve them in order of rank. Navy, marines, air force— I learned to count the stars." Prior to one banquet, Glen made a list of guests so he could keep them straight. "I kept the list for years."

The general's dining room, like other temporary structures, was a canvas tent with a peaked roof. Tent sides could be raised into awnings to provide light and ventilation, but flaps of the general's dining room stayed closed for privacy and to keep an astonishing number of insects at bay. The kitchen, noisy with gas burners, occupied a tent fifty feet away.

Glen served high-ranking officers food similar to that consumed by the average marine: rehydrated eggs, beets, onions, and corn; plus potatoes, rice, and beans. He recalls, "There were no dairy products, fresh vegetables, or meat, except lamb from New Zealand." He and a fellow waiter from Chicago, Joe Walkoz, presented the main course on platters, which they held to an officer's left as he served himself. When Glen and Joe melted into the background, nary a dropped napkin—or word—escaped them.

Glen's family back in California had no idea he could have described in detail the U.S. strategy for winning the war in the Pacific and which islands the generals planned to use as stepping stones to Tokyo.

According to Maureen, "we didn't get letters too often, and when we did, parts were cut out."

Like all letters written by GIs, Glen's were censored. His were read by the general's aide. "You couldn't even say that you were on an island or that it rained often," Glen says. "That was giving away too much."

Maureen recalls, "At mealtimes, when the news was on the radio, we didn't talk because we wanted to learn the whereabouts of the Marine Corps."

Ruth planned meals to conserve rations of beef, butter, and sugar. She also displayed a satin banner, embroidered with three gold stars, in a front window. "We were so proud," Maureen says. "One star was for Glen, another was for Deloris, then we added a third when Merrill joined the army."

Although Glen did no cooking while on Guadalcanal, he learned to estimate how much food would be needed based on the number of people to be served. "You didn't need much rank to get supplies. You said, 'the general needs this or that,' and you got it."

The head cook, a sharp-featured marine with a sour disposition, ignored pleas from Glen and Joe for a worker to wash dishes. In a letter home, Joe wrote: "Dear Mom, we're up to our ears in dirty dishes, and we really need an extra person to help out."

"Sure enough," Glen says, after the general's aide read the letter, "we got a dish washer."

As Glen and Joe cleared china plates and poured coffee, Vandegrift might cause a ripple of laughter among his subordinates by confessing he "didn't even know the location of Guadalcanal" when it was assigned to him.

Geiger, whose deep crow's feet attested to hours of squinting into the sun, would cloud the tent with cigar smoke as he discussed strategy. Glen recalls, "His aides joked about how a pilot once flew over New Zealand and parachuted cigars to the general."

When all had vacated the dining tent, Joe and Glen slid into seats once occupied by men whose decisions would change the course of history. "And from there," Glen says, "we ran the war." Joe, a skilled mimic, duplicated Vandegrift's solemn pronouncements, the way Geiger jabbed the air with his cigar, and Halsey's bulldog stare.

But when an exuberant Joe, while ladling food in the mess tent, performed his presidential imitation ("Mah son Jimmy hates wah, mah wife Eleanor hates wah, I hate wah"), "it embarrassed me," Glen says. "I knew Vandegrift was a friend of Roosevelt, and even though the mess tent was noisy, I knew the general could hear."

In the fall of 1943, Glen heard Geiger's plans to take control of the island of Bougainville, north of Guadalcanal. As smoke from his cigar curled into blue haze, Geiger described the landing in boxing terms: "a series of right jabs to throw the enemy off balance, and to conceal the real power of our left hook to his midriff at Empress Augusta Bay."

Glen's unit was sent to Bougainville, then back to Guadalcanal, and later, after the battle of Saipan, to Guam. On the way to Guam, to avoid enemy submarines, the ship followed a circuitous route through the Philippine Sea. It eventually arrived at the Marshall Islands, a staging area, where it took on supplies.

"We knew the end of the war had to be near. When we anchored, as far as you could see, there were aircraft carriers, destroyers, battleships, and more."

To alleviate boredom during an ocean voyage that lasted six weeks, Glen played poker with several fellow marines. The players kept a record of their earnings and losses, and planned to settle up when they returned to the ship after the Guam landing.

When at last they arrived at Guam, Glen recalls, "All night long, the battle wagons fired, and planes came in. The bombing went on and on. It was like the Fourth of July. It was a spooky feeling, just before dawn, when all the firepower stopped to let the first wave of marines go ashore. Then we watched the boat come back with some of the wounded."

Several hours later, it was Glen's turn to climb down ropes and drop into a landing boat. On shore, "mostly I saw dead Japanese. We took very few prisoners. We were warned, 'If a Japanese has a hand grenade, he'll blow himself up and you, too. Also, Japanese snipers would climb the trees at night. Even though they were totally exposed, and knew they were going to get it, they'd take the chance."

During three weeks on Guam, Glen was assigned guard duty. "One night, I got under a palm tree, which seemed like a nice secure spot. Then the moon came out, and I felt like I was on stage. I couldn't relocate. Nobody was supposed to move, even to go to the restroom." A coconut fell from the tree, and a dog made a rustling sound in the brush. "They were nothing, but I'll never forget the fear."

Another night, he trained his M-1 rifle on a shadow that moved along a trench between tents. Moonlight revealed a fellow marine who evidently hadn't heard Glen's whispered request for the current password: "Babe Ruth." Glen recalls, "When I didn't get a password, I was supposed to shoot. It was a close call. I can still feel the trigger against my finger."

After thousands of Americans and many more Japanese died on Guam, the Japanese resistance surrendered in August 1944. When Glen returned to the ship, "It looked a lot better than when we left it. You can't get any sleep in a foxhole." But when the poker players met to settle up, some were missing. Glen mourned his friends, then felt relief when he heard they might have been assigned to another ship. "We never did find out what happened to them."

In August 1945, when Glen and other servicemen learned the United States had dropped atom bombs on Japan, "We felt sad at the loss of lives but also relieved. We thought of all the servicemen who would have been killed if we had landed in Japan. It would have been a bloody mess."

As the war wound down, Glen was sent to China. "I have no idea why," he says. "But I do know we were the first Americans to land there. We went up the river to Tientsin on barges. A few of us rented rickshaws and were pulled through the streets, to the delight of curious onlookers." As the crowd parted, "We'd wave like we were generals."

Although their futures were uncertain, Glen and his fellow marines sailed homeward in a state of euphoria, anticipating the welcome of relatives and friends. Across the U.S., families sifted every sound, whether footfall or car door, for hints of long-awaited homecomings.

Ruth knew Glen was home when she heard the shrieks and squeals of her teenage daughters. When her son's large frame filled the kitchen doorway, she wiped her hands on her apron and took a deep breath.

"You just relax," Ruth said as Glen hugged her. "I'm fixing your favorite dinner, fried chicken with biscuits and gravy and mashed potatoes."

Shortly after Deloris and Merrill also returned, Maud Johnson's suffering came to an end. According to Deloris, "Grandma was laid to rest next to Grandpa Johnson at Cherry Mausoleum in Long Beach."

The Bell family became fragmented after the war. Glen's parents and his youngest brother, John Richard, moved back to Cedar Springs. Maureen and Dorothy, Deloris says, "were sent to Long Beach to live with Aunt Clara and Aunt Anna (Bell), because there was no longer a school for them to attend in Cedar Springs." Deloris married a former air force sergeant, and Merrill went to work for the Army Corps of Engineers in New Mexico.

Glen returned to San Bernardino where his best friend, Neal Baker, offered him work. Before the war, Neal and his brothers had built a family home with bricks they made themselves from clay soil mixed with straw. In 1946, they opened an adobe brickyard and sold the heavy earthen bricks for thirteen cents apiece. They needed someone to haul their product, and Glen agreed to do it for five cents a brick. He bought a 2.5-ton army surplus truck with two axles. Not long afterward, Neal says, "We went broke when new government regulations required that adobe bricks be reinforced with steel."

Glen sold the truck and went to work as a "car apprentice," restoring and rebuilding freight cars for the Santa Fe Railroad, San Bernardino's largest employer. A welding job in San Bernardino during the summer "was about as hot a job as you could find," Glen recalls.

"Fifteen minutes before quitting time, things quieted down," he adds. "The workers cleaned their tools and put them away. They wouldn't wait to hear the factory whistle; they'd start moving when they saw steam start to come out of it. One minute after quitting time, there was nobody left. I figured, if that group liked their jobs that well, I sure didn't want to make a career of it."

As he evaluated his skills in terms of San Bernardino's booming postwar economy, Glen often met Neal for lunch at Mac and Dick McDonald's prosperous E Street drive-in. But before he could plan a course of action, Glen, like many ex-GIs during the late forties, fell in love.

Glen's Recipes for Success

#13: Sometimes what you don't say is more important than what you do say.

I've always been on the quiet side. Some believe that's a liability in business, but I always found it to be an asset. When people know you'll keep your mouth shut, they're more likely to confide in you. And when you listen instead of talk, you learn.

#14: Any job is an opportunity to learn.

You would think that serving food to generals in Guadalcanal wouldn't have much relevance later on. But it taught me how to estimate how much food was needed based on the number of people served. That knowledge gave me confidence to start a restaurant. Even menial work holds lessons you can build on—if you look for them and put them to use.

#15: Choose a career that truly interests you.

Jobs were plentiful after the war, and I tried several on for size. As a welder for the Santa Fe Railroad, I worked with men who dropped their tools when the whistle blew. I knew that spending my days waiting for the shift to end wasn't for me. The pay was good, but I wasn't using my talents or creativity, and that to me was more important.

CHAPTER FIVE

Bell's Hamburgers
1947-1949

WHEN GLEN BELL WAS TWENTY-FOUR, he decided to do two things he didn't realize would conflict: to own his own business and to marry a girl he now admits was "way too young."

Dorothy Taylor was seventeen when she met Glen, and eighteen when they married. If Dorothy could tell her story today, it's likely she'd say she felt ready to have her own home and family. Her own mother, after all, had married at sixteen. Glen was mature and stable, Dorothy's parents liked him, and no doubt she didn't want to return with them to Texas. Southern California, sizzling with postwar prosperity, was an exciting place to be.

Bernard Taylor, Dorothy's father, remembers his only daughter as "a beautiful blonde, a real pretty girl. I have a picture of her on the mantel, and I look at it every day." Today the elderly widower is retired from farming cotton and corn. He brought his family to San Bernardino during World War II "so I could work at the air force base. Glen Bell met Dorothy, and they were seeing each other real regular. We really learned to love Glen Bell. After we moved back to Texas, we'd go out to San Bernardino and spend Christmas with them."

In contrast to Glen, Dorothy was outgoing and talkative. No doubt her Southern accent and the way she made his name two syllables (*"Glay-en"*)

American Restaurant Magazine

San Bernardino, 1948. Parking lot of the original McDonald's. Glen built his first hamburger stand four miles away to avoid infringing on what he considered Mac and Dick McDonald's territory.

charmed him. With America in a marrying frenzy—his friend Neal already had succumbed—it seemed pointless to wait.

Mrs. Johnson told Glen about a small house for rent in an older section of San Bernardino. "I got it for eighteen dollars a month," he recalls. "After the war, I was lucky to get anything. Without a place to live, we might have postponed the wedding." The ceremony, in Las Vegas, "wasn't anything complicated. Dorothy's folks were leaving for Texas about the same time."

Glen worked as a meter reader for Southern California Gas and soon became as captivated with a vacant lot as he had been with Aunt Mary's bakery. The property was on the border of San Bernardino and the industrial city of Colton, across the street from a public swimming pool. Daily, after work, Glen visited the lot, and as he paced the unimproved parcel, he imagined its potential as "a place for families to go to have fun." He told Dorothy he envisioned a miniature golf course and asked her opinion on placement of tiny bridges and buildings, and where customers might park and enter.

Glen spent four hundred dollars to lease the lot for a year. At the time, his salary was $150 a month. He soon realized he lacked funds to build a miniature golf course and began to consider less expensive options.

Neal Baker remembers when Glen decided to build a restaurant: "We were sitting in our cars, with our wives, in the parking lot of McDonald's Drive-In."

American Restaurant Magazine

San Bernardino, 1952. The McDonald brothers: Mac, center; Dick, right.

It was obvious Maurice ("Mac") and Richard ("Dick") McDonald, both in their forties, earned an excellent income. Glen recalls, "You could look in the carport behind the restaurant and see their new Cadillacs." The brothers had receding hairlines and round, jolly faces. In photos taken at the time, they also have similar smug smiles.

Neal adds, "Dick was married, and Mac lived with them. Neither had children. Mac told me they started out with an orange juice stand in Monrovia (a suburb of Los Angeles)." In 1940, the brothers moved the juice stand to San Bernardino and converted it to a carhop drive-in. "McDonald's" prospered, and seven years later, the brothers shared a twenty-five-room mansion with a view to the southwest of San Bernardino's palm-lined streets. For recreation, they attended boxing matches.

Their best-selling item was hamburgers. Glen's location, four miles south, didn't infringe on what he considered their territory.

Once again, Glen's teenage wife watched him pace and plan. He envisioned crowds of eager customers when the public pool reopened in the spring. All he needed, he told Dorothy, was a simple concrete-block building with a kitchen, cash box, and order window. He would create a restaurant reduced to its basic elements: a hybrid of a drive-in and a sidewalk cart. He would take orders himself, prepare simple but quality food, and hand it to customers so fast they wouldn't miss being served by a waitress. There would be no seating, indoors or out. Customers could stand at a front counter or eat in their cars.

Today, people assume that walk-up, take-out restaurants always have existed, but in 1947, except for sidewalk carts, no eateries sold fast food— including the McDonald brothers. "It was either indoor service or carhops," Glen recalls.

If Dorothy had been pleased when he used an employee discount to buy a deluxe gas refrigerator—an item hard to come by after the war—she no doubt was disappointed when he sold it to pay for building materials. Glen asked his best friend how to "poor-boy" the construction, and Neal made several money-saving suggestions, such as placing the restroom, drink station, and sink all in one line.

Glen recalls, "We spent long evenings discussing whether to save by making the building twelve feet wide instead of sixteen feet, so we could use two-by-fours instead of two-by-sixes." He obtained a line of credit from a neighboring lumberyard and used it to buy construction materials, cabinets, and hardware.

Glen learned how to pour cement and lay concrete block by watching laborers construct a grocery down the street. As he built his stand, "I must have looked like I knew what I was doing, because people who saw me work offered construction jobs, and I made a few extra dollars on the side."

He didn't know how to put in electrical wiring and plumbing, "but I did it anyway. I ended up with a lot of pipes and wires exposed. Building inspectors weren't as tough then as they are now. In fact, while I was laying block, an inspector who stopped by offered to give me a hand."

Glen purchased a grill on credit from Murray's Restaurant & Hotel Supply in Colton. For fifteen dollars he bought an old-fashioned ice box that required a block of ice daily. Just before Glen opened "Bell's Hamburgers" in March 1948, he quit his job at the gas company, and he and Dorothy moved into an apartment next door to the restaurant.

As Glen awaited the summer reopening of the Colton Warm Water Plunge, with an anticipated daily attendance of five thousand, he perfected his kitchen's efficiency and "researched" menu items by eating at other restaurants. He decided his next major purchase would be a root beer machine because the drink's brisk sweetness perfectly complemented juicy hamburgers. In the meantime, he sold bottled soft drinks. "They were a hassle. I'd stack them near the restroom, and they'd break. And the empty bottles had to be returned."

Employees of neighboring stores patronized his walk-up restaurant, but the summer crowds Glen anticipated never materialized. Headlines warned of a disease that caused crippling bone defects in children, and because the virus—known as "polio"—could be spread through water, "attendance at the plunge dropped to nearly zero."

It helped to be on a busy street, but customers, accustomed to carhops, sat in their vehicles and waited for someone to come and take their orders. When they honked for service, Glen motioned them to the window. Fortunately, those who protested the minor inconvenience soon complimented him on how quickly the food arrived. "They expected to stand and wait fifteen minutes."

He adds, "Customers also liked not having to tip and not having to dress up to eat out. Back then, if you had work clothes on, you didn't go into a restaurant." Instead of packing sandwiches in lunch pails, construction workers bought nineteen-cent hamburgers at Bell's.

Business gradually increased. "It meant working long hours just to make a bare living. I stayed open until the last customer was gone. I'd get there at 9 A.M., open at 10, and stay until 1 in the morning." In June, the McDonald brothers visited, ordered burgers, and discreetly observed his operation.

Because he used an icebox, Glen had no way to keep perishables overnight. He saw this as an advantage, however, because fresh-bought ingredients meant better-tasting food. His experience ordering supplies overseas came in handy as he estimated how much meat, lettuce, and cheese to buy daily.

"You'll get better food at a busy restaurant," he advises. "With a high-volume operation, the ingredients move quickly and tend to be fresher."

During July and August, temperatures soared past one hundred degrees. Glen's shirt became soaked with sweat, and the icebox overflowed. Dorothy sympathized, and in her soft Southern accent, urged him to go back to work for the gas company.

By summer's end, he had earned enough to pay his debts. Dorothy pointed out that they now could afford a nicer apartment. Glen replied it was more important to correct errors he'd made in the restaurant's construction and design. "The parking lot was dirt, and every afternoon I had to wet it to keep the dust down. Also, the counter was too short and faced the sun and wind."

Glen waited until business diminished in the fall because he thought construction would deter customers. "I learned it doesn't matter. Making improvements doesn't chase anyone away. Action creates more action. People will place their drinks on an unfinished wall." He spread gravel on the parking lot, extended the counter, and used four-by-four posts to build a framework for a ten-foot awning. "When it was done, it was beautiful. I was really proud of it."

Two weeks later it was ruined. "Eighty mile-an-hour winds came through one night. I woke up in the morning, looked out the window, and saw the awning and posts wrapped around a telephone pole. Looking back on it, it wasn't really that much. But at the time, I was really discouraged. I wondered what to do, whether to just give up. I had spent everything."

During the days that followed, Glen was silent, withdrawn, and unable to plan a course of action. The solution seemed obvious to Dorothy, and she urged him to look for a job with predictable hours and a steady, dependable income. He told her he had committed to a year's lease and paid for the restaurant's equipment.

About the same time, the McDonald brothers closed their prosperous restaurant—temporarily. The drive-in, less than a half mile from San Bernardino High School, had become a hangout for rowdy teens. According to Neal, "Mac and Dick couldn't make the carhops do what they wanted." Signs announced that an improved McDonald's would open in December.

The next unexpected news was that Dorothy was pregnant. "It was nothing we'd planned," Glen says. "I was surprised—pleasantly, of course." She informed Glen she wanted a larger home in a suburban neighborhood, and a husband who came home at 6 P.M. and didn't work weekends.

"Her friends were married to men with regular jobs, and she wanted what they had," Glen says.

But Bank of America had approved his application for a fifteen-hundred-dollar loan, and Glen now had the means to repair his hamburger stand. Again, he paced and made pencil sketches on scraps of paper. As he totaled columns of numbers, he realized he also could afford to put a down payment on a root beer machine.

He recalls, "You mixed sugar, concentrate, and water in five-gallon stainless steel buckets, then poured the mixture into a forty-gallon tank that carbonated and refrigerated the root beer. It came out smooth and creamy, not highly carbonated, with a nice foamy head. It was sweet, but didn't fill you up." He persuaded an ice cream supplier to lend him freezers, which he used to chill mugs.

Glen also added hot dogs to the menu and built a candy bar rack. Even so, the changes he made were modest compared to those happening across town.

When the McDonald brothers' restaurant reopened in December, it included two walk-up order windows and a reorganized kitchen designed to crank out hamburgers, assembly-line style, in advance of customers' orders. They had streamlined the menu to a few popular items, and incredibly, in a time of rising prices, reduced hamburgers from thirty to fifteen cents. China, silverware, and carhops were gone. To further emphasize the concept of quick service, they renamed their mascot, a neon-cartoon chef, "Speedee."

A few months later, Glen also opened a remodeled hamburger stand. Sales averaged twenty-five to thirty dollars per twelve-hour day, but business increased as the weather warmed.

"I can still see the counter lined with ice cold mugs. Kids loved it. Root beer foam would spill over the sides, freeze on the glass, and they'd lick it off." A glass of root beer cost 1.2 cents to make; Glen sold it for five cents.

He discontinued the candy bar rack. "It's bad business to spend time making next to nothing. Candy bars sold for a nickel; there was two cents profit. It wasn't worth it. On a nineteen-cent hamburger, the profit was 50 percent."

By summer, sales tripled. His fifteen-year-old sister, Dorothy, returned from Long Beach, stayed with Glen and his wife, and went to work for him. She recalls, "It was fun for me, my first job."

Glen had learned to make a perfect hamburger, and he made sure his sister did, too. "The hard thing is judging how long to cook the patty. No two are the same," he says. "One minute, two minutes, every batch of meat is different. Wait until the patty is two-thirds cooked before you flip it over. Then there's very little to finish."

Glen adds, "We'd start the day with four or five hundred hot dogs. The stack really impressed people. When it got busy, we'd continually move the hot dogs from the warm end of the grill to the middle, where they cooked, then along to the other end, where they stayed hot."

Hot dog buns came six to a box, and he reused the boxes to package food orders. "With a fifteen-cent item, you really have to watch your costs. Using the boxes not only saved us money, it reduced trash."

Just when the stand was busier than ever, and Glen could take no time off, his wife gave birth at the local hospital. They named their son Rex.

When Glen's wife again reproached him for his long hours, he promised to sell the restaurant at summer's end.

His sister turned sixteen that same month and announced her engagement to her boyfriend, Douglas Thorley. She had additional news for Glen: Her future in-laws were interested in buying his business—if he could prove it was profitable.

Glen recalls, "The Thorleys were not too sure the figures I had for them were right. So I invited them to come on Saturday and stay all day. That evening after we closed, we counted the money." The cash box was heavy with change, and the crash it made as he poured its contents onto the dining room table seemed to last forever. Glen and the Thorleys stacked coins for half an hour. The total came to four hundred dollars.

Cedar Springs, 1949. Glen and his first wife Dorothy take their infant son Rex to visit Glen's mother. The Pontiac is new; Glen paid three thousand dollars for it after he sold his first stand.

"It had been a good Saturday, one of the biggest days we'd had."

After the Thorleys paid $6,900 for the restaurant, Glen took his wife shopping for a new car. Her delight in the new blue Pontiac sedan made up for his misgivings at spending three thousand dollars.

Because Dorothy didn't want a self-employed husband, Glen's next challenge was to find a job with regular hours and a steady paycheck.

Glen's Recipes for Success

#16: Respect your competitors and learn from them.

At first, no one, not even the McDonald brothers, fully recognized the potential of fast food. But we did know, because of the customers' response, we were onto something. We experimented and continually made changes. Our "market research" was to observe our competitors and to borrow their best ideas.

#17: Overcoming problems is part of attaining a goal.

When a windstorm destroyed the improvements I'd made on my hamburger stand, I almost gave up. What I didn't realize at the time is that disasters invariably happen when you're building a business. If you expect them, it's easier to take them in stride.

#18: Customers are drawn to a store that is busy, growing, and changing for the better.

I was surprised people came to my hamburger stand while I was remodeling it. It gave me a good feeling when I watched them set their drinks inside hollow concrete blocks, on top of an unfinished wall. I discovered that construction doesn't chase customers away. Action creates more action. People like the feel of success.

CHAPTER SIX

Beyond the Burger
1950-1952

AS GLEN DROVE THE STREETS OF SAN BERNARDINO and neighboring communities looking for "Help Wanted" signs, he noticed a miniature golf course for lease in Fontana, a town that had grown around the Kaiser Steel Mill.

The course had closed during the war and needed paint and repairs. Glen lost track of time as he envisioned the parking lot cleared of weeds and packed with cars owned by steelworkers. He could hear their children's laughter and smell the popcorn he would sell them.

"I leased the miniature golf course," Glen recalls. "But it was terrible. It made the food business look good. Fontana was a steel town, and all those guys wanted to do was drink beer. Golf was a sissy game."

His sister Dorothy says she and her husband would park their car in the lot "to make it look busy and try and attract customers. We'd sit around with Glen and talk. Quite a few times Glen asked, 'Do you have any ideas for making money? There has to be a way. If you sell enough of anything and make a profit on each one, even if it's a penny apiece, if you sell them fast enough you'll make a million dollars.' We weren't as interested. After a while we'd say, 'OK, Glen. Let's talk about something else.'"

Her in-laws, the Thorleys, made a lot of friends, Dorothy says, but the hamburger stand they bought from Glen didn't prosper. "Whenever a customer asked for something, they added it. So before long, they were selling homemade chili, candy bars, and chips. It was too many things, too much work, and not enough profit."

Glen adds, "One thing I learned from the McDonald brothers is, don't sell everything your customers ask for. Decide what you're going to sell, then make it the best it can be."

Glen gave up the miniature golf course and once again agreed with his wife that he shouldn't try to own and operate his own business. Yet when he applied for a job at a service station, "The whole time I was talking to the owner, I was thinking about how I could build a hamburger stand across the street."

The site was the corner of a market parking lot at Mt. Vernon and Oak, on the outskirts of San Bernardino. "I made a deal with the boys who owned the grocery store to pay twenty-five dollars a month rent. They said we could use their restrooms. I was about to pour cement when a guy from the Health Department chewed me out because of no restrooms. I had been trying to stretch money left over from the sale of the first stand, and a restroom added five hundred dollars to the cost."

Glen's best friend Neal adds, "Glen had no money, but he managed to talk Mr. Murray (of Murray's Hotel & Restaurant Supply) into financing $3,500 worth of equipment for nothing down. You'd never see that today. And the building probably violated all kinds of codes. Glen didn't even have a suction fan." Soon after, Neal himself paid a visit to the surprisingly generous Mr. Murray and built a hamburger stand of his own on Highland, three miles north of Glen's and two miles east of the McDonald brothers'.

"Neal and I were friendly competitors," Glen says. "By then, there were lots of people doing the same thing."

Around the same time, according to Glen's older sister Deloris, "Daddy left Cedar Springs, leaving twelve-year-old John Richard with Mom."

His father's actions confirmed what Glen already had decided: "I knew I didn't want to be like him. I felt bad for my mother, but I also felt in many ways she was better off without him." Glen never again saw his father, who moved to New Mexico. After his divorce from Ruth was final, Glen Sr. remarried. He died in 1978 at age eighty.

With her twenty-seven-year marriage ended and no source of income, Ruth moved to San Bernardino, enrolled in nursing school, and went to work part-time. To his regret, Glen was unable to help his mother financially. "But people expected me to. They think because you're in business, you have money." Also, his wife Dorothy "wasn't too anxious to help. It was all she could do to stretch our money to pay for groceries and rent."

As Glen had done earlier, the McDonald brothers were busy proving that customers required neither carhops nor sit-down service. Lunchtime lines at their remodeled restaurant were twenty customers long, and the tiny octagonal kitchen's counter-to-ceiling windows revealed a remarkably efficient crew. Kids and would-be competitors stood outside, sipped soft drinks, and watched with the rapt attention of theatergoers.

Mac and Dick introduced several innovations that Glen and Neal observed with interest. Glen recalls, "I used to take buns out of the wrapper, slice them, then slide them back inside the bag to keep them fresh. The McDonalds got a bakery to put sliced buns on big wood trays, then they covered the buns with waxed paper."

They also used a machine to form patties. "The meat came hard, semi-frozen. They used an ice cream scoop to place a ball of hamburger between sheets of wax paper, then flattened it with the pull of a handle."

To make their french fries look appetizing, Glen adds, "the McDonalds installed big mirrors and infrared lights." The innovative lighting kept the fries crisp and warm and also enhanced their golden color. Mirrors, positioned at an angle above the french fry bin, made the food visible to customers.

The brothers solved the problem of serving drinks in bottles that had to be returned, or glasses that needed to be washed: They introduced paper cups. Disposable cups were sold in stores but were yet to be found in restaurants. "I thought that was the greatest thing ever," Glen says. "You pull a handle, fill a cup, and you're done with it."

Neal recalls the McDonalds' custom-made "goopers"—hand-held stainless steel pump dispensers for catsup and mustard. According to an article in the July 1952 issue of *American Restaurant* magazine, "With a thumb control, these efficiently provided an exact, controlled amount of condiments for each bun." The cover story's headline was: "Take-Out Trade: twelve-by-sixteen-foot restaurant space sells one million hamburgers and 160 tons of french fries a year."

Mac and Dick McDonald, Glen adds, also helped their competitors by educating the general public that self-service take-out food, sold at bargain prices, could be high quality. Earlier, people had assumed lower prices meant an inferior product.

Though his business did well, Glen realized San Bernardino soon would be saturated with hamburger stands. He became caught up in the idea of selling a different product with comparable appeal, but he had little time for research. Even when his sales volume justified hiring an employee at a dollar an hour, Glen hesitated to leave. "I felt I couldn't afford to lose a single customer. I didn't want to see one bad hamburger go out."

When Glen at last felt confident his employee could handle the business, he visited one of San Bernardino's many Mexican restaurants. Tacos were among the *antojitos*, or appetizers, and were served soft or crisp. Glen observed

San Bernardino, 1998. A commemorative plaque is all that remains of the original McDonald's Drive-In.

that regular customers placed a warm tortilla across the palm of one hand, spread the tortilla with shredded meat, doused it with salsa, and rolled it. As they ate the soft taco, they folded the end with one finger to keep the sauce from dripping. Since tortillas were the Mexican equivalent of bread, Glen wondered why no restaurant made tacos assembly-line style—like delicatessen sandwiches or take-out hamburgers.

Glen told his wife he thought crisp-shelled tacos, if he could find a way to make them fast enough, would be an ideal menu addition. Dorothy opposed the idea. Not only was Mexican food too spicy, she told him, the stand did just fine with hamburgers. Why take a risk and make a radical change?

Also, by then most of their friends had moved to homes in new suburbs north of town, and Dorothy may have assumed that introducing Mexican food would keep them in a small apartment in a Hispanic neighborhood near downtown. In any case, she did not trust Glen's business acumen or encourage him to pursue his idea.

Glen agreed with Dorothy that the baby needed more room, and a move to the suburbs was desirable—but he told her the timing was not yet right. He asked her to be patient.

He used their savings to rent a vacant lot on Mt. Vernon at Sixth, across the street from a tortilla factory. The property was 50 by 125 feet, and the ground lease was fifty dollars a month. With Neal's advice and hands-on help, Glen began construction.

The two friends continued to notice every change made by the McDonalds. Glen recalls, "They installed microphones for customers to use when ordering, and we thought, oh, boy, that's great. We'd had a problem with talkative customers. They'd tell you their life story. You can't just drop them when another customer walks up." Because people who had to speak into a microphone would be reluctant to chat, Glen assumed it "would take away the personal element."

Glen changed his mind, however, when he observed a fat little boy scream into a microphone at McDonald's, "Gimme a cheeseburger!" Everybody inside jumped.

When he completed the new restaurant, Glen found a married couple to operate the small stand on the corner of the market parking lot; they paid him a percentage of sales.

Six months later, he sold that restaurant to finance yet another. He had observed how Mac and Dick offered french fries at a building separate from their hamburger kitchen, and realized he had space to do the same at Sixth and Mt. Vernon. "They did five thousand to six thousand dollars a month just in fries," Glen recalls. "That's about what we were doing with everything." A second food stand on the property would increase sales volume but "wouldn't cost any more rent."

Dorothy asked if he ever intended to use business profits to improve their family's lifestyle. Glen again asked her to be patient and described his plans to sell Mexican food—along with fries and malts—from the second building. He believed he had arrived at a crucial point in his business, one that could lead to an operation comparable to that of the McDonalds."

Glen's first challenge, during taco-making experiments, was to create crisp shells ready to be filled. He found he could dip a tortilla in hot fat and it would hold its shape, but when he folded a tortilla in half and fried it, the sides stuck together and then shattered when he pried them apart. He experimented with a stainless steel holder with two parts, one to cradle the tortilla, and the other to fit inside the folded disk and separate its edges. "I bent metal to make forms to hold tortillas open while they fried. But stainless steel stays hot and can burn your hands."

A basket made of wire worked better, and because it didn't compress tortillas, the shells came out lighter and crisper. "I worked with an equipment salesman who contacted a man who made chicken coops. He made a fry basket for me out of chicken wire." The basket had a handle, and was constructed to hold six folded tortillas at a time. A second wire basket fit over the first to hold the tortillas open and in place.

He modified his chili-dog sauce to flavor taco meat and also use as salsa. "I mixed tomato puree with chopped fresh onions, garlic, cayenne pepper, vinegar, and Mexican spices—and left out the Liquid Smoke."

Glen's next challenge was to hold shells upright in his taco assembly line. A narrow V-shaped metal trough about two inches deep and eighteen inches long seemed ideal. His "taco slide" worked well at first but became clogged with melted cheese. To create a holder that would allow excess taco filling to fall out of the way, Glen positioned parallel steel rods over a metal tray. "But the opening was too wide on the first set I made, and not only did surplus filling fall through, the tacos fell through, too. I made another 'taco rail' real fast the day before I introduced them, and it worked fine."

Tacos sold steadily that day, but after closing, Glen had misgivings. "There were so many pots and pans dirty, I was there until three in the morning still cleaning up. I thought, 'what have I gotten myself into? This is a big mistake.'"

As weeks passed, however, Glen found tacos less messy than other items. "When you fry hamburgers all day, the grease is in your hair; it's even on top of the refrigerator. You cook taco meat in one thirty-pound pan. It bubbles rather than sizzles, which makes a big difference."

Tacos had other merits Glen had not anticipated. "With hamburgers and hot dogs, each order is different. One person wants cheese, another tells you to hold the onions. During a rush, you have to keep track of five or six orders at a time while watching the meat on the grill to make sure it doesn't overcook. With tacos, every order is the same. It's quick and easy. You can assemble tacos and hand them out as fast as people order them."

Before long, he hired a full-time taco maker, and Bell's Hamburgers and Hot Dogs became the tortilla factory's best customer. "Of course, tortillas weren't as popular as they are now, but our little stand went through more tortillas than San Bernardino's largest chain of supermarkets."

Glen noticed his Hispanic neighbors ate *frijoles* with every meal, so the next step was to introduce creamy refried beans. They made a tasty and nutritionally sound accompaniment to tacos made of corn tortillas, meat, cheese, and lettuce. He bought dry pinto beans by the sack at nine cents a pound. "When you added water and cooked them, they tripled their weight, so we were really getting them for three cents a pound." Customers who paid nineteen cents for an eight-ounce order of refried beans considered it a bargain, yet beans were a high-profit item.

Beans, however, had a labor-intensive drawback: Small stones often were packaged along with them. "The stones looked just like the beans," Glen recalls. "You needed good light when you sorted through them. We went through a hundred pounds of beans a day, and never had a customer complain. But we always worried about it."

In 1952, profits from Glen's "fast-service" Mexican food paid for a down payment on a house on Marshall Boulevard, in a tree-shaded suburb north of town. At first, Dorothy was satisfied. Then old problems resurfaced. The restaurant was still Glen's mistress.

"Anybody who wants to go into business for himself has to realize it takes you away from home duties," Glen admits. "Especially if you're operating a restaurant. If you want to work only eight hours, you might as well not go into it."

On the other hand, "If you don't put time into your business, it can be worse for your family in the long run, because you're not able to pay the bills."

Having a husband who was self-employed didn't make his wife feel secure, Glen adds, "but I felt as much security as I would have had if I was working for someone."

Bell family archives

San Bernardino, circa 1952. Glen helps his son Rex assemble a train set.

The final straw was when Dorothy asked Glen to come home early on Rex's birthday. Although Glen said he'd try, by the time he arrived, the little boy was in bed. Dorothy was furious; Glen was silent. Both realized their differences were irreconcilable.

Bernard Taylor, Dorothy's father, recalls, "It like to killed us when they split up."

To make sure his son's needs would be met, Glen gave Dorothy the house, their bank account, and his only source of income: the two stands on one lot at Sixth and Mt. Vernon.

"My thought at the time was I could start over," he says. "But it bothered me when she bought a new Mercury. I was driving an old pickup. The money could have gone into the business."

Glen's Recipes for Success

#19: Volume is the key to profit.

There was no shortage of mom-and-pop restaurants in the fifties. Many served good food, and a few introduced the carryout concept. But those that grew into chains also had low prices and quick service. Quality food, speedy service, and low prices created demand. This led to greater volume, which in turn generated greater profits.

#20: Don't let even one bad order go out.

No matter how large your business becomes, its reputation depends on the counter help. I saw to it my employees consistently prepared a product that was up to my standards, and treated customers as welcome guests. The continued growth of the business depended on it.

#21: Don't sell everything customers ask for.

It's important to please customers, but that doesn't mean you should try to sell all things to all people. Instead, work hard to improve your area of specialization. You'll beat the competition when it comes to quality and expertise. Customers will come to you because they want the best.

#22: The best ideas often are the most simple.

In the 50s, the race was on to create a better take-out burger. Rather than re-invent the wheel, I applied quick service to an entirely different product. Tacos beat burgers when it came to taste and speed, yet were simpler to prepare and serve.

CHAPTER SEVEN

Taco-Tia
1953-1956

IN 1953, WHEN HE WAS THIRTY, Glen moved seventy miles east of San Bernardino to a tiny desert town located on the two-lane highway that led to Las Vegas.

Before air-conditioning became commonplace, few places to live were more miserable in August than Barstow. And during the 1950s, the town was as remote as it was inhospitable.

Barstow, Glen says, "was three hours out of L. A. It was where people stopped to get gas." Travelers were hungry, and in the intense heat of a Barstow summer, thirsty too. Glen obtained a bank loan and built a fast-food restaurant similar to those he had owned in San Bernardino. The site he selected was a block east of the largest Standard Oil gas station in the United States.

He also chose Barstow because it wasn't San Bernardino. "Since I gave the stand on Sixth and Mt. Vernon to my ex-wife, I didn't want to stay there." He planned to offer solely Mexican items, "but at the last minute I was afraid tacos wouldn't sell outside San Bernardino, so I added hamburgers."

On the night before the eatery opened, "hardly a car went by. I thought, boy, this is a loser." Yet the business soon exceeded Glen's goal of a hundred dollars a day. Consumers had become accustomed to fast food and looked for it when they traveled.

Fast food as an industry was prospering. Glen's best friend Neal Baker opened a second take-out restaurant in Rialto, between Fontana and Colton. And in San Bernardino, the McDonald brothers' daily sales topped a thousand dollars.

For $950, Mac and Dick sold Ray Kroc, a restaurant equipment sales-man, the right to open a McDonald's in Chicago. But except for A&W Root Beer and ice cream vendors Dairy Queen and Tastee-Freez, franchised eateries were uncommon.

With profits from the Barstow store, Glen leased a small hamburger stand in Indio, a desert town in Riverside County. To help his mother with her finances, Glen gave it to Ruth, who operated it with Glen's seventeen-year-old brother, John Richard.

When tacos outsold hamburgers in Barstow, Glen concluded an all-Mexican fast-food restaurant would succeed in any area with good traffic flow. He scouted locations in cities surrounding San Bernardino and sketched the floor plan of an improved restaurant on graph paper. The eatery's grand opening, he decided, would be a giant party. In his imagina-tion, Glen heard Mexican guitars and the clicking of castanets, and saw dancers twirl in colorful ruffled skirts. He commissioned an art student to draw the restaurant, and included the drawing in his business plan.

Glen realized credit might be difficult to obtain because he had yet to settle debts related to building the Barstow store. Yet he was confident oth-ers would share his dream once they understood it, and he visited several banks. No loan officer was interested. One told him if tacos were such moneymakers in Barstow, he eventually would accumulate enough capital to build whatever he wanted. That, however, would take several years. Glen was determined to proceed with his plan—before someone else beat him to it.

In search of moral support, Glen visited a friend who owned a variety store in south San Bernardino, Al McDonald (no relation to the McDonald brothers). Al was small and wiry, twenty-five years older than Glen, and quick to voice an opinion. When Glen described his concept and showed him the drawing, Al told him, "I'll pay for it—if we can be equal partners."

Glen recalls, "Al wanted to get out of the variety store business. The neighborhood was a bad one for petty theft. He had a one-way mirror in his office, and he was always catching someone. But he was on the easy side, and he'd let them get away with it. I helped him liquidate his inventory."

The art student had named the conceptualized restaurant "La Tapatia." Al suggested they shorten it to Taco-Tia. The name was easy to say and remember, but must have perplexed many Spanish-speaking customers; the literal translation is "Snack Aunt."

Al's grandson, Tod McDonald, remembers his grandfather as "a very determined individual with a strong work ethic. He could be cantankerous, but he was always kind. He'd give poor people a handout."

Glen moved from a boarding house in Barstow to an apartment a block away from the new restaurant's construction site. It was on Baseline Street, adjacent to the largest supermarket in town, about a mile west of the McDonald brothers' hamburger stand.

During construction, he visited his ex-wife's home to see their son. Her boyfriend, Kenneth Sharp, met Glen at the door, told him to leave, and threatened to have his car towed away. Glen's sister Dorothy recalls that he was hurt and dismayed; after all, when they divorced, Glen had given his wife all their assets.

With his dream restaurant under way, Glen had little time for a social life. Women were not a priority with him—but two unmarried school-teachers made him theirs.

They lived in apartments in the same building as his and belonged to a figure skating club that met at the Orange Show Fairgrounds. When they invited him to the rink, Glen accepted. He found its cool interior a welcome change from the hot San Bernardino sun, and after a few lessons, he discovered that he had a natural gift for skating. The group, which included several more teachers, was friendly, and Glen felt at ease when it came time for ice dancing. Lights dimmed as the first notes of music echoed throughout the cavernous building, and couples holding hands glided into position.

When asked what first attracted him to Marty Ahl, a twenty-five-year-old teacher who lived with her parents, Glen replies, "her interest in tacos."

No doubt he also noticed Marty's deep blue eyes, her pleasant smile, and the way she wore her thick brown hair in a wavy bob. She was tall and graceful and, as their skates moved in unison, fit perfectly within his six-foot-two frame. Marty had a comfortable, confident way about her, and Glen liked the way she listened. When he spoke, she would lower her chin and look up at him with a gaze that promised undivided attention and an intelligent response. As Marty described the trials of substitute teaching at local junior highs, Glen savored her good nature, quick wit, and common sense.

San Bernardino, 1954. Martha ("Marty") Ahl was a schoolteacher when she met Glen. Her mother Ellen was a dietitian and teacher; her father Harl was a civil engineer.

Marty and her parents had come to Southern California three years earlier. "San Bernardino was a beautiful little town surrounded by orange groves," she recalls. "The mountains in the distance turned pink at sunset, and there was one main street with a neat little shopping district."

Her parents had earned degrees from Purdue University; her mother was a dietitian turned schoolteacher, her father was a civil engineer stationed at Norton Air Force Base. "His name was Harl L. Ahl, a German name,"

Marty says. "You can imagine what it was like to spell that for a long distance telephone operator."

Marty spent her early childhood on a farm her parents had owned during the Depression, near Indianapolis. "My dad would get up in the morning, put on boots and overalls, and go out and feed the animals. Then he'd change clothes, put on a suit, and go into town as a consulting engineer."

It amused Glen when Marty told him she had retained a fondness for chickens. "They're such sweet little creatures. On the farm we had a flock of chickens, three hundred in the spring."

During the war, as Harl transferred to various bases, "we lived all over the South. Tampa, Biloxi, New Orleans, Ft. Leavenworth, Colorado Springs, Shreveport, and back to Meridian, Mississippi, three times. We enjoyed seeing the country, and we got so we could move quickly. We had a tiny bit of household goods." Wherever they lived, Marty's mother Ellen easily found work as a substitute teacher. Marty followed her mother's lead and earned a teaching credential from State College in West Texas in 1951.

In California, Marty's salary was four hundred dollars a month. "I was making so much money I bought a car."

Harl taught his only child how to use tools and never to discard anything of value. Marty recalls, "He'd go to a garage sale, and there'd be a box of hardware. He'd buy the whole thing for a dollar, then come home and organize all the items in glass jars. He could pull out any size screw, hook, or nail. Once I brought him a flashlight that didn't work. He drilled it out, found a new switch he'd been saving, and it worked good as new."

On their first date, before he escorted Marty to dinner at a Mexican restaurant, Glen met Ellen and Harl. Marty says her father, who by then had retired from the air force, liked Glen. "My dad was intrigued by what he was doing, building the taco stand."

A few months later, the Mexican take-out restaurant Glen envisioned became a reality.

His brother Merrill recalls, "Glen bought an old two-ton bread truck and thousands of straw hats from Mexico." Each *sombrero*, woven from

San Bernardino, 1954. Mariachis and Mexican dancers transformed the grand opening of Glen's first Taco-Tia into a colorful fiesta. Glen (top center) and his partner, Al McDonald (far left, back row), wear two of the free hats given away that day. Two tacos and a drink cost forty-eight cents.

strips of palm, had fringe that extended outward ten to twelve inches. Hand-painted letters on the upturned brims spelled "TACO-TIA."

Glen instructed his brother to tack hats onto the outside of the truck, then drive to the stand. "I was supposed to pass out free hats when I got there, but every time I stopped at a stop sign, kids tore hats off the truck," Merrill says. "By the time I got to the grand opening, about half the hats were gone. But as it turned out, it was the best advertising."

Glen agrees. "Up and down the street, people were wearing our hats."

That evening, searchlights illuminated Glen and Al's taco stand and announced its presence to greater San Bernardino. Merrill recalls, "Glen put up a platform and hired a *mariachi* band to play Mexican music." Hispanic men in gold-embroidered jackets strummed guitars and violins, and sang, "*ai-yai-yai-yai, canta no llores.*" Women wearing embroidered blouses, full skirts, and colorful woven belts raised their arms, clicked castanets, and laughed as they danced. But no smile was broader than Glen's beneath his fringed sombrero as he sold nineteen-cent tacos as fast as he and his employees could assemble them.

"I knew we had a winner," Glen says. "We grossed around eighteen thousand dollars the first month."

According to Marty, "The stand started out well. In San Bernardino, Mexican food wasn't unusual or exotic, it was inexpensive and good, and a Mexican restaurant was where you went out to eat. At Taco-Tia, two people could eat for under a dollar. It was such a unique little stand—you'd go to a public event and hear people talking about it."

Glen recalls, "Marty used to come by Taco-Tia after school, between three and four. We'd talk and make a date for later. I'd swear I'd be on time, but the place was doing so well, I couldn't get away. I'd say, 'I'll try to be there at seven,' but I'd get there at nine."

He also had little time to supervise operations at Bell's Hamburgers in Barstow, and the stand suffered as a result. Glen asked a part-time employee of Neal's, a serviceman stationed at George Air Force Base, to become the stand's manager. Ed Hackbarth had a friendly demeanor and a ready smile, and Neal attested to his dedication to hard work and customer service. It didn't bother Glen that Ed had been fired earlier from Bell's Hamburgers and Hot Dogs at Sixth and Mt. Vernon. Dorothy's boyfriend had taken over the store and dismissed all employees except the full-time taco maker.

Ed recalls, "He said it was his 'policy' to start over with all new people."

The twenty-two-year-old was newly married. He told Glen he didn't mind leaving the air force to work full time, but he knew his wife wouldn't want to live in the desert. Glen says, "I told Ed I'd sell him half the business if he'd stick it out in Barstow."

Ed remembers Barstow as "a small city with huge train yards. The temperature was always over ninety degrees in summer, and it was even hotter inside because we had to keep the meat and grill hot." Though dust storms were frequent, "they didn't keep customers away." Even so, he added a glass enclosure to the front of the stand.

Glen taught Ed to excel in fast service and how to manage a half dozen employees. "Glen told me, 'Even though you do 70 percent of your sales from 10 A.M. to 6 P.M., the 7-to-midnight employees can ruin your business.' "

Ed was outside washing windows one night when Glen stopped by. "Glen tapped me on the shoulder and asked why the manager was doing janitorial work. I said, 'Glen, you know I'm not washing windows, I'm watching employees.'"

That spring, Glen changed the name of the Barstow store and sent Ed thousands of straw hats with TACO-TIA emblazoned on the brim. "Glen paid ten cents apiece for them. We threw them from a truck during the Barstow Rodeo Days parade and caused a traffic jam. Everyone in town wanted one. The next year, they wouldn't let anyone throw anything."

In Barstow, tacos sold for twenty-five cents each. "We still sold hamburgers," Ed recalls, "and added *tostadas*. My record was fourteen Mexican-food orders per minute. We also fried taco shells daily."

Nearly a decade later, in 1964, Ed founded a fast-food chain that currently has three hundred outlets throughout Southern California: Del Taco.

"I helped several of my competitors get started," Glen says. "People seem to think we ought to hate each other, but we've stayed good friends."

Glen's friend Neal Baker also recognized the profit potential of Mexican fast food and added it to his menu in 1955. The thirty-one Baker's Burgers Neal owns today in San Bernardino and neighboring communities are unusual in the fast-food marketplace because they offer both Mexican and American fare. Each store averages nine hundred thousand dollars in annual sales, and Neal is a multi-millionaire.

Today, as in the mid-1950s, cities surrounding San Bernardino share an oasis-like ambience. In parks and along avenues, towering king palms resemble those of a pharaoh's palace. Alongside highways grow verdant jungles of pepper trees, oleander, and menthol-scented eucalyptus.

Glen found ideal locations for Taco-Tias in neighboring Riverside and Redlands. His partner, however, argued that there was no guarantee that additional Taco-Tias would do as well as the first. They should quit while ahead and keep the profits instead of risking them. But when Glen urged Al to reconsider, he relented. The new restaurants "were so successful, we paid for the building and equipment in the first six months."

Bell family archives

Redlands, California, circa 1955.

They rented a vacant grocery store in San Bernardino to warehouse restaurant supplies and to prepare food items such as refried beans and tortilla shells. Though the commissary increased their overhead, it ensured product quality and uniformity. Al bought paper goods and other items at quantity discounts—sometimes by the truckload, because he didn't want to disappoint the salesmen.

Redlands also was home to the Los Angeles Rams football team's training camp. "They had big appetites," Glen recalls. "One football player might order and eat a dozen tacos."

Two players were so fond of tacos, in fact, they asked Glen if they could open a similar store in downtown Los Angeles.

McDonald's franchises were beginning to spread across the country, and Glen decided to test the concept. "I sold a Taco-Tia franchise to Charley

Toogood and Tom Fears. They were football heroes, and their enthusiasm was exciting."

Because the Redlands taco stand was on State Highway 99 midway between Los Angeles and mountain ski resorts, it also attracted rich and famous customers. According to Tod McDonald, "My grandfather told me they had a collection of bean cup lids with celebrity autographs. John Wayne was one of them."

Yet success had its downside, Glen says. "You could stand outside and look right along our assembly line. One night during rush hour, it was probably Friday, I looked out the window and saw a man's face. He was so intense, the way he was watching, I knew I'd see him building a taco stand." Sure enough, six months later the man opened a restaurant called "Taco Tio" in Los Angeles.

Even so, Glen's heart was light. Marty had agreed to marry him. He proposed to her early in March 1955, but neither remembers the exact moment. According to Glen, "It may have been in the parking lot of a Taco-Tia."

"We were engaged two weeks," Marty recalls. "Back then, people didn't have long engagements. We had a very small wedding in the Presbyterian church on E Street. I didn't buy a new dress because I didn't need one, but I might have bought new shoes. I wore a beautiful suit (skirt and jacket) with long sleeves with cuffs. My mom and dad were there, and Glen's mom, and his brothers Merrill and John Richard."

The newlyweds drove to Northern California, stayed in the coastal village of Carmel south of Monterey, then continued north along the Oregon coast. When they returned to Glen's apartment, the unmarried schoolteachers next door, Marty says, "were dismayed to see me move in."

"It changed their prospects," Glen adds with a smile.

That summer, the Bells rented a cottage in Running Springs, a mountain community northeast of San Bernardino, for sixty dollars a month. Glen recalls, "The cottage was surrounded by pine trees, and there were several hundred steps leading up to it." In the evenings, they watched the sun set over the Los Angeles basin, and in the mornings, looked out over a serene sea of coastal fog.

According to Marty, "The sun would warm the big veranda. We'd sit outside and drink coffee and watch the sun melt the clouds that filled the canyons."

That same summer, the McDonald brothers again remodeled their San Bernardino eatery, this time with two neon-illuminated "golden arches" on either side of the building. The grand-re-opening, Glen says, "was a warm, sticky night. We all went out to see it. The McDonalds hired every searchlight in town, fifteen of them, and all those lights attracted bugs. I drove down the street, and beetles crunched under the tires of my car. When we got out of our cars, we walked through bugs. Inside, fly fans were throwing them against the windows. The brothers had to close early."

Also that summer, Disneyland opened in Anaheim, a city south of Los Angeles. "It was surrounded by miles and miles of citrus, grapes, and wineries," Marty says. "Before that, amusement parks were traveling fairs with pitch-penny games. Disneyland was beautiful, and there were cute kids in costumes just dying to talk to you because so few people were there. I remember thinking how popular it would become when people discovered it."

San Bernardino, circa 1955.

At Disneyland, on opening day, Glen lost track of time as he contemplated the park's small-scale buildings, turn-of-the-century downtown, Victorian-era steam locomotive, and flower-filled landscape. Disneyland reminded him of the miniature golf courses he had hoped to develop, yet Walt Disney had expanded the concept of a family-oriented park into a realm Glen had yet to imagine.

A few weeks later, Glen realized his tendency to lose track of time could be dangerous. To facilitate trips to Barstow and Indio, he had obtained a pilot's license and bought a small plane for seven hundred dollars.

"I was so determined to get where I wanted to go, I'd go when I shouldn't. I was out one afternoon with an equipment supplier, and I didn't realize how late it was until it started to get dark. I didn't want to fly at night because the plane had no lights or radio, so we made an emergency landing in a wheat field on top of the Cajon Pass." Marty drove to the remote location to pick them up. Soon after, Glen sold the plane.

A pork roast persuaded Glen to buy a house in Redlands. "When we went to look at it, the lady of the house had a roast going in the kitchen. It smelled really good. There was a fire in the fireplace, and the house had a glassed-in family room with a view of San Bernardino. We bought it for $13,500."

In November, Marty gave birth to a son, Gary; and Ruth, now known as Grandma Bell, came to live with them.

The Ahls also bought a house in Redlands. "In the garage my dad built an overhead structure full of hooks to hold extra lumber, wire, sheeting, and even old sunhats," Marty recalls.

With a tidy income from three restaurants and his family settled and comfortable, Glen easily could have justified no further business expansion—especially since his partner was opposed to it.

But Al's reluctance "really went against the grain," Glen says. "I knew if we didn't develop the product's potential, someone else would."

"Glen was a lot younger," Tod McDonald says. "My grandfather didn't want to take the gamble." Glen sold his share of the partnership to Al, who eventually mustered the courage to open several additional Taco-Tias.

His grandfather, Tod adds, accumulated "a few million dollars in assets and could live any way he wanted, but he owned a small house, wore bib overalls, and drove a truck." Al died in 1991; today Tod operates seven Taco-Tias in the San Bernardino area.

Once again, Glen gave up the successful restaurants he had created and faced starting over. This time, he would seek his fortune in Los Angeles.

Glen's Recipes for Success

#23: Pick a location based on your customers' needs, not on your own comfort.

An ideal location for a fast-food restaurant is several hours from a major metropolitan area, on a highway that leads to another city or recreational area. Our stand in Barstow attracted customers who were hungry, thirsty, and ready to stop. It was miserable in the summer without air-conditioning, and an inconvenient place to live, but the sales volume was worth it.

#24: See to it that the whole town knows you're in business.

Opening a business is an occasion to celebrate, so invite your customers to share the excitement. We used music, dancers, free gifts, and searchlights to attract attention. People stopped to see what was going on, and pretty soon our grand opening turned into a giant party. Customers felt welcome, enjoyed our food, and returned with their friends.

#25: Work with those you believe in and believe in those you work with.

In order to grow, you have to trust your employees. Sometimes people would steal from me, which was sad and disappointing. But I believe that the more you train and encourage people, the more they feel a part of the business. And people generally don't steal from their own businesses.

CHAPTER EIGHT

Celebrity Partners
1957-1961

HOW, GLEN WONDERED, CAN YOU GO WRONG with a fast-food restaurant on Pasadena's busy Colorado Boulevard?

"Traffic was thick and slow at all hours," Glen recalls. Every evening, commuters transformed the four-lane street into a white river of light. He estimated ninety thousand cars per day—three times the number that passed the Taco-Tia in Redlands. Yet sales lagged.

When Al bought Glen's share of the partnership, Glen retained the right to use the Taco-Tia name, with the understanding he would not build competing restaurants in San Bernardino or neighboring communities. Daily, Glen drove sixty miles west to Los Angeles. With a coffee-stained map spread across the front seat next to him, he cruised busy streets, visited realty offices, parked in front of eateries, and watched customers come and go.

If a site seemed promising, Glen visited it repeatedly. "You want to know what's going on at different times. A location that's busy at noon might be dead at nine at night. I used to count cars at 2 A.M." A taco stand, he adds, should do the same volume of sales from opening to 6 P.M., and from 6 P.M. to closing.

"Night business depends on the menu. With a hot dog menu, you cater to a different customer, one who wants a snack, not dinner. Mexican food can be lunch, dinner, or a snack."

Of many excellent properties available, Glen narrowed his choices to two: one on Pacific Coast Highway in Long Beach; another on world-famous Colorado Boulevard, the site of the annual Pasadena Rose Parade. "I bought the land in Long Beach and leased a building in Pasadena." He planned to use profits from the Pasadena Taco-Tia to build a new one in Long Beach.

But in the 1950s, people patronized restaurants much less than they do today, and were less inclined to order take-out food. "Dinner was something you went home to, not something you picked up on the way," Glen recalls. And eateries had yet to offer the convenience of drive-through service.

The problem with Colorado Boulevard, Glen adds, was "the quality of the traffic. You'd see cars lined up before getting on the freeway, but those people were in a hurry to get home or to work. They didn't want to stop for anything."

Pasadena's work force also was a disappointment. Marty recalls, "So many people came and applied for jobs, but when you saw them, you'd just despair. One time, fifty turned up for a part-time janitor job, and none looked like someone you'd want to give a key to."

In January 1958, a clean-cut college student approached Marty as she hosed the parking lot of the Taco-Tia on Colorado Boulevard. John Galardi had arrived in Pasadena with his family the week before, and earlier that day all four family members headed down the boulevard, determined to find work.

John recalls, "My mom, dad, and brother got jobs. I looked for six hours, telling people I'd do anything, with no luck." On the way back to his family's apartment, he saw Marty.

She says, "I liked John because he seemed quick and bright. He was nineteen and had come all the way from Missouri." When Marty followed John inside, "I stood behind him, held up a job application and waved it at the manager."

Months earlier, when Glen had told Marty he planned to end his partnership with Al and start over with a new Taco-Tia in Pasadena, she had just settled into the spacious home they had bought in Redlands, not far from her parents. Her son Gary was a newborn. Yet without hesitation, Marty prepared to move.

"Otherwise Glen would have had to drive back and forth, and we'd see him every week and a half." Grandma Bell moved with them into an apartment in Pasadena. She looked after Gary while Marty kept the books and worked at Taco-Tia.

On January 1, the Bells enjoyed front-row seats for the Rose Parade. Marty recalls, "We put an easy chair on the blue line, the line they paint on the street for spectators. Grandma Bell sat in the chair and held Gary in her lap. As the parade went by, there were so many flowers, and they smelled so good, it was like burying your face in a bouquet."

Because the Pasadena store did not provide the profits he had hoped for, Glen became determined to build on his Long Beach property. Drivers who passed the vacant lot on Pacific Coast Highway included commuters, but the majority were area residents and customers of neighborhood shops. Also, business likely would surge on weekends and during the summer. The lot bordered Atlantic Boulevard, a busy north-south route to the beach, and was within sight of a two-story motel.

Glen considered borrowing money, "but the economy was in a recession, and I was reluctant to go into debt."

Though wary of partnerships, he was tempted when approached by Charley Toogood. Before he was traded to the New York Giants, the former L. A. Rams tackle had co-owned a Taco-Tia franchise in downtown Los Angeles. He and Glen also were friends.

It was a "thrill of a lifetime," Glen says, when he was Charley's guest during a game at the Coliseum. Glen sat on the bench with the players. "There were eighty-five thousand people yelling. I heard Rosie Grier say a few choice words when he came back from making a play."

Charley's widow, Ginger Toogood, says their unusual surname originated in England. Charley, she adds, "grew up in Nebraska—he's in the state college hall of fame—and was drafted by the Rams the year they were world champions."

At the Taco-Tia in Redlands during training camp, "Charley fell in love with Mexican food." After six years in pro football, he retired in 1957.

Charley's lifelong friend, former L. A. Rams linebacker Harland Svare, recalls, "Charley liked to eat, and he liked Glen's idea of duplicating the McDonald thing with tacos. In those days, pro football players worked during the off season. Our salaries were only six thousand to eight thousand dollars a year. Charley sold insurance, but he enjoyed being around food, and he liked the restaurant business."

Glen got along well with Charley and envisioned how his football-star status might be used to promote a restaurant. But Charley had only ten thousand dollars to invest.

Charley persuaded Harland to join them. He says, "My nickname's 'Swede.' I'm from a tiny fishing town in the state of Washington. I hadn't heard of Mexican food before I came to California. I ate my first taco in 1953, when I was twenty-three."

Harland brought in a fourth partner, Phil Crosby, the son of singer/entertainer Bing Crosby.

Phil and Harland had met at Washington State University. "I went out for the freshman football team," Phil says. "Our team was cannon fodder for the varsity. I had two speeds, slow and slower, but I had great lateral movement. A scout went to Washington State and saw Harland. He was six-one, weighed 225, and played a great defense."

Harland adds, "I was on the varsity and played both offense and defense, which was unusual. In pro football I was a linebacker."

Phil was the youngest of the four partners, and his famous father asked Harland why he wanted Phil to join them.

Harland says, "I was honest with Bing. We wanted to use the Crosby name and capitalize on it. Bing said, 'Go ahead. That's what it's for. Use your football names, too.' We had some photos taken for promotional use, but never got around to using them."

The photos Harland refers to were taken at the Long Beach construction site of Crosby, Svare, Toogood & Bell's first "El Taco," on the same summer day Glen met Phil. At five-eleven, Phil is not as tall as the others, but his short-sleeve knit shirt reveals an athlete's build.

"I worked out with weights and weighed 215," Phil says.

In contrast to the others, who have dark brown hair, Phil's is white-blond. Behind the four men, on Pacific Coast Highway, are cars with tail fins. Visible through the coastal haze, on a distant ridge, is a spindly forest of oil derricks. These rise above Signal Hill, where Glen's grandfather, Ed Johnson, had made a fortune brokering real estate thirty years earlier.

Long Beach, circa 1957. Partners Harland Svare, Phil Crosby, Charley Toogood, and Glen Bell at the construction site of their first El Taco.

Glen transferred ownership of the Long Beach property to the partnership, and the new restaurant did even better than he anticipated. Their overhead, however, was high.

Glen recalls, "We leased a seven-thousand-square-foot commissary big enough to serve a hundred stores. We paid seven hundred dollars a month rent, hired a manager and bookkeeper, bought a truck and hired a driver, paid salaries to three partners—and we were building new stores." Glen and Charley worked for El Taco full time. Harland, who had been traded to New York, worked during the off-season.

Phil recalls, "Harland was so proud of the commissary, he was like a new father showing off his first-born. I was tremendously impressed. I thought the commissary proved Glen had foresight and wisdom. The place prepared food and made taco shells, sauce, and beans. It wasn't some little place; it was bigger than anything I had seen in the army."

When Glen expressed concern about costs, Harland and Charley reminded him that through Crosby family connections they had access to venture capital.

"I told them, 'Yes, if we show we're doing the right thing.' I wanted to go easy on the expenses and show a profit the first year." The partnership also benefited from Bing's attorneys and business advisors—up to a point.

Glen had hired twenty-year-old John Galardi to manage the commissary. "It was chaos," John says. "Employees were working eighteen-hour days, and the owners drove the trucks on weekends. I got it down from fifteen to twelve people, and they worked fewer hours. Then a consultant came in and told the partners, 'Why are you paying a kid $150 a week?' He advised them to cut my salary in half."

When John gave notice, Neal Baker hired him for two hundred dollars a week to work at a Baker's Burgers in Los Angeles. Glen also shook his head when consultants informed the partnership the commissary made money on taco shells and lost money on beans; he knew the opposite was true.

Except for Glen, "none of us were businessmen," Harland admits. He adds he "did whatever was needed" at the commissary, including deliveries. Accompanied by Phil, Harland also "checked on properties," which meant visiting El Tacos to inspect the sites and evaluate food and service.

Phil recalls they drove to the various locations in his car. "It was a Chevy Impala, curved instead of high tail, a copper-bronze color, two-tone with a white top. Even though it was a coupe, it was roomy enough for the two of us. Harland and I used to call it 'running the gauntlet.' We'd start at the El Taco at Hollywood and Western, nearest my house. We'd go in, have a taco, talk to the people who worked there, then move on to check the next property."

All the partners scouted sites for new stores, which eventually numbered "seven or eight," according to Harland.

Ginger Toogood recalls, "We used to go out looking for locations with Glen and Marty, while our little girls slept in the back seat. We'd be out until 2 A.M. We enjoyed Marty and Glen so much. And it was such fun when Glen opened stores with searchlights and mariachis."

Harland and Charley visited a one-room real estate office on Pacific Coast Highway owned by Bob Trujillo, a slender twenty-seven-year-old of Hispanic heritage. "These two big guys walked in," Bob says. "They were

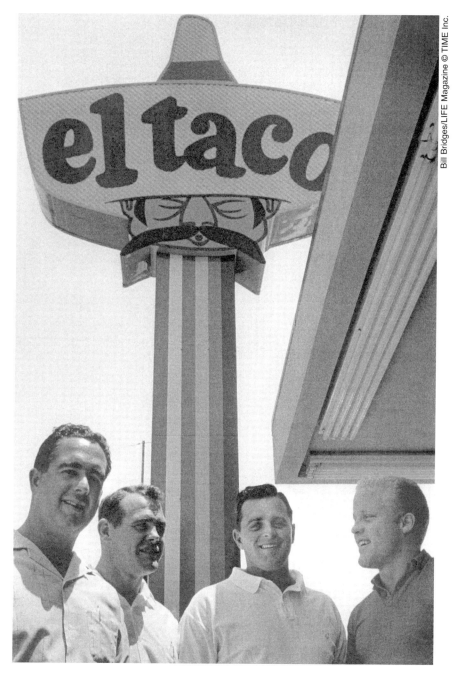

Los Angeles, 1958. El Taco partners Charley Toogood and Harland Svare were pro football players with the Los Angeles Rams. Glen is on their left; entertainer Phil Crosby (Bing's son) is on their right.

El Taco partners toast each other in another photo taken by Life *magazine.*

so big they filled the office. They couldn't fit into the chairs. They told me they wanted a location for a taco stand in Wilmington."

Then, as now, the south Los Angeles suburb sits on a vast pool of oil, and the air smells of hydrogen sulfide and tar. In the mid-1950s, oil pumps were everywhere, even in the yards of tiny tract houses, and their motion was constant. On the end of a rocking steel beam, each pump had a wedge-shaped counterweight that resembled the head of a praying mantis; extending from the mandible was a slender rod that pierced the ground. The El Taco partners agreed that Wilmington's population of blue-collar refinery workers, longshoremen, and their families were ideal fast-food customers. Bob recommended a vacant lot next to his office.

When Glen viewed the location, he told Bob he preferred a corner lot across the street. Bob didn't argue, even though the lot had a rental house on it. "I could see Glen was special and different," Bob says. He persuaded the property owner to tear down the house. When the new El Taco opened, it was a hit; Glen's instincts had been on target.

"It was a ten-year lease for $450 a month," Bob recalls. "My commission was 3 percent of the rent for ten years, which came out to $13.50/month. I went home happy, because I had half of my own rent paid for ten years."

Bob adds, "From that day on, Glen and I became close. He liked me, I guess because I was young, honest, and naive. Glen was the most unique person I ever met. He had imagination, creativity, dedication—and no clock. I'd tell my wife, 'Glen's here,' and she knew she wouldn't see me for two or three days. He had no conscious awareness of time. He worked eighteen-hour days, seven days a week. He'd keep going by drinking coffee. He was single-minded, and he never committed to a schedule."

Bob, who speaks Spanish, accompanied Glen on a trip to Mexico. "Glen loves the Mexican culture, with its music, bonfires, and the way they create a warm, happy, festive feeling. He wanted to see pots, designs, and colors. In Mexico City, when he saw the flower boats of Lake Xochimilco, he wanted to build a floating Mexican restaurant."

When asked why they went to Oaxaca, a province of mountain villages, Bob waves his hand. "Because it was in the middle of nowhere, I suppose, and Glen was always taking a different approach to things. He liked to sit in the square, the *zocalo*, and watch people go by."

In the summer of 1958, Phil and his three brothers formed The Crosby Brothers quartet. He recalls, "When we were kids, one of Dad's associates from a radio show taught us to sing basic harmonies." *Life* magazine decided to do a cover story: "Bing's Boys: Ready for the Big Time."

"*Life* followed us around for a couple of months. They photographed us in front of our house on Mapleton Drive in Holmby Hills. It was a hot day, but we wore striped suits and boaters and held canes."

El Taco partner Phil Crosby presents a tostada.

The photographer accompanied Phil to an El Taco and took photos of the four partners beneath the restaurant's sombrero-shaped sign; in front of an order window, toasting one another with soft drinks in paper cups; and surrounding Phil as he leaned across the counter, one arm extended,

The only photo of the partners used by the magazine. According to Phil Crosby, Life's *visit to El Taco was the first (and last) time he worked in a restaurant. (This photo reproduced from magazine copy.)*

presenting a tomato-laden tostada. In these three photos—which were given to Phil, but did not appear in the magazine—Harland, Phil, and Charley have wide, confident grins.

Glen's smile is shy, and his gaze doesn't quite connect with the camera. "I knew the magazine was there to photograph celebrities, not me."

Only one photo of the El Taco partners accompanied the article. It shows all four wearing the white paper hats of food preparers. The men are aligned near stainless steel bins of shredded lettuce, cheese, tomatoes, and cooked ground beef. Harland, at the far end, leans forward, his hands behind his back, and looks down the assembly line. Charley holds a taco shell in one hand and a scoop of filling in the other. Glen nestles cheese atop a tostada on a six-rod taco rail in front of him. Phil—who never before had worked in a restaurant—is in front, turned to face the camera. He holds a taco between his fingertips.

The article appeared in September, and the Crosby brothers opened in Chicago the following spring. Their act was a hit, Phil says. "One segment was a medley of Dad's tunes, 50 songs. We'd sing two lines from one song, then go on to two lines from another." They were booked at Chez Paris in Chicago, and then the Sahara Hotel and Casino in Las Vegas. "By the time I got back, we'd built two more stores."

That same month (March 1960), Marty gave birth to a daughter, Kathleen. Thirty-seven years earlier, Glen had been born in the same Los Angeles hospital, in the suburb of Lynwood.

Phil brought his new wife, a Las Vegas showgirl, to a meeting the El Taco partners held at the Brown Derby restaurant in Hollywood. Glen recalls Phil's wife was a redhead with beautiful legs. "In Hollywood, people don't pay much attention if a woman's nice-looking, but she got glances. She seemed pleased Phil was doing something outside the entertainment field."

Los Angeles, 1960. Glen and Marty and their children, Gary and Kathleen.

Bell family archives

As the meeting progressed, Glen adds, "I was really happy. With all that overhead, there shouldn't have been any profit, but we managed to come out ahead. Charley reported, 'We did nineteen thousand dollars at the Long Beach store.'

"Phil asked, 'Is that gross or net, Charley?' I thought nineteen thousand dollars gross for a nine-month period was great, but Phil's question took the wind out of Charley's sails."

When Phil and Harland learned the net profit was a mere $3,500, Glen recalls, their faces fell. "It didn't sound like big money to them." While on the road, Phil had averaged $1,600 a week.

Glen adds, "There were four of us, so whatever we made was split four ways. Yet I suffered the same and worked as hard as if I'd been the sole owner."

After two years, he sold his interest in El Taco to his partners for what he had put into it: ten thousand dollars. Glen sold for no gain, even though the chain was growing and doing well.

"I signed the papers, they took on all the liabilities and profits, and that was it," he says. The breakup "was no reflection on them. They were good partners. But I had a strong desire to be independent. There were no hard feelings. An attorney told me 95 percent of partnerships don't last over two years."

Soon after, Harland also sold his interest in El Taco. "Football was where my heart was. I knew running a restaurant business wasn't what I was going to do with my life. I left when I was offered to replace Tom Landry as a coach of the New York Giants."

If he had it to do over again, Harland says, "I'd tell Glen, 'do whatever you want to,' and let him do it. When Glen went on to found Taco Bell, I took a lot of needling." Harland currently operates his own fitness consulting firm at a health clinic north of San Diego.

"I was on the road all the time," Phil gives as his reason for selling his share.

For a few years, Charley continued to operate El Taco in partnership with his brother and brother-in-law. After Charley sold them his interest, he moved his family to Ginger's hometown, St. Helena, California, where they operated a drive-in owned by her father.

Ginger adds, "Charley also coached high school football, which he found very rewarding." Charley died in 1997 from complications of diabetes.

At present, according to Ginger, "There are two El Tacos in Downey, one in San Pedro, one in Orange (all in the Los Angeles area), and one in Tennessee. Jerry Toogood, Charley's brother, owns all five."

Phil recalls, "After we were bought out, I didn't see Charley and Glen personally, but Harland would call them from time to time. I was working a lot in Indiana and different places. I led a vagabond life and blew a couple of marriages. In the sixties I worked service clubs around the Pacific Rim. I lost touch. Then all of a sudden, Taco Bell was everywhere. I knew it was a tremendous success, and I was happy as hell for Glen."

Phil adds, "I never regretted a minute of the El Taco partnership. Later we wished we had stayed with Glen, but we can't knock ourselves. It was a good experience. In the photos the three of us are grinning like we'd won the lottery."

Glen's Recipes for Success

#26: It's not the quantity of the traffic that counts; it's the quality.

Too often a restaurant's location is based on the amount of traffic. But if drivers are in a hurry to be elsewhere, they won't stop. Commuters who passed the Taco-Tia on Colorado Boulevard, for example, were hurrying home from work. Stores in Redlands and San Bernardino had less traffic flow, yet did better business. They attracted people who were cruising around after dark and wanted a snack or were on their way to the mountains from L. A.

#27: When you have a setback, learn from it and plan your next move accordingly.

I knew it wasn't the product's fault that the store on Colorado Boulevard didn't do as well as I had hoped. Earlier restaurants had proved there was a market for take-out Mexican food. Once I figured out the problem was the quality of the traffic, I was confident a different location would solve it.

#28: If you must take a partner, choose as carefully as you would a spouse.

Twice I entered into partnerships because I needed operating capital. Neither worked out, even though my partners were good people. We just didn't share the same vision or the same degree of dedication to the business. Each time, in order to regain control of my dream, I sold my share of the partnership and started over.

CHAPTER NINE

Early Taco Bell
1962-1964

THE RACE WAS ON. Glen was confident he could create a profitable chain of fast-food Mexican restaurants. What he didn't know was whether he could do it before the competition beat him to it.

"Winchells opened Taco Fiesta and built four or five restaurants," Glen recalls. "Fosters also had a Mexican concept. Taco-Tia and El Taco had a head start. All of them had more resources than I did."

Despite evidence that tacos had carved a niche in the fast-food marketplace, no loan officer shared Glen's enthusiasm. To raise money, he sold the restaurant on Colorado Boulevard and also a vacant lot he owned near Bob Trujillo's office in Wilmington. Glen's father-in-law, Harl Ahl, bought the latter.

"Glen had leased it to a guy who put eight trampolines on it," Bob says. "Day or night, you could look across the street and see people bouncing up and down. Glen used to sit and smile and get a big kick out of it."

Glen easily convinced friends, relatives, and acquaintances of the potential of Mexican fast food. "But I wasn't a good closer. I built up to it, but I couldn't ask people for their money." Although desperation helped him overcome this, his reticence led him to offer generous terms.

John Galardi recalls, "Glen said if I'd give him $6,000, in ninety days he'd pay me back $9,000. I told him in ninety days he could pay me back $6,000. I was twenty-one and bomb-proof."

Three friends of Bob Trujillo's also lent Glen money. "Each put in $4,000 for a total of $12,000," Bob says. "Glen agreed to pay 100 percent interest a year until he paid them back. So one year's interest was $12,000."

Bob found sites for six restaurants, but because Glen couldn't afford to pay commissions, he gave Bob 1 percent of each store's gross "for the term of the lease and any extensions," Bob recalls. "I said to Glen, 'Is that good?' He said, 'You don't realize.' It was about 10 percent of the stores' net profit. It was like an annuity. They're all expired now, but I held on to those agreements for twenty years."

At a time when every penny was precious, Glen's expenses escalated during construction of a taco stand in south Hollywood. The site, across from CBS at the intersection of Beverly and Fairfax, was commercially ideal. It also was near the La Brea Tar Pits. Then, as now, sticky black goo oozed from low-lying ground—and occasionally alongside sidewalks—throughout the area. "The ground is very unstable," Glen says. "We had to put pilings down forty feet."

In Wilmington, "the trampolines went out of business," John Galardi recalls. "Glen felt bad because he had sold his father-in-law the lot." Harl wanted to build a take-out restaurant on the property with Glen's help, but Mexican food was not an option because of the El Taco nearby. Glen suggested hot dogs, an item that had sold well at his fast-food stands in San Bernardino, and John agreed to operate the restaurant. "I figured I'd do the McDonald's of hot dogs."

Over dinner one evening, John, Glen, and Marty discussed names for the new stand. John recalls, "We considered John's Hot Dogs and Wonderful Hot Dogs. Marty had been looking through a cookbook earlier that day and said, 'You should call it Der Wienerschnitzel.' I thought, can you imagine? What a stupid idea. Then I remembered a marketing class I took in college, about how the human mind acts as a filter; it screens things out that aren't meaningful. You don't notice things that aren't important to you. You buy a brown Ford, and all of a sudden you notice brown Fords everywhere you go. I figured if people would drive by and see this unusual name, they'd ask, 'What is that?' Pretty soon it would be burned in, and they'd recognize it."

He adds, "We sold three types of hot dog—a mustard dog, a kraut dog, and a chili dog—each for fifteen cents. Drinks were ten cents. We used the same chili sauce recipe Glen had used at his hot dog stand. We blew the competition away."

There was no formal agreement between Glen and John, but both understood the business belonged to John. Glen says, "I helped him get started, but he did all the work."

John recalls, "I'd get to work at eight in the morning and leave at 1 A.M. or 2 A.M. the next day. I'd work every day, and on Sunday I'd open the store and take the afternoon off."

John credits Bob Trujillo's friend and one of Glen's early investors, Bill Lindner, for persuading him to add Polish sandwiches to the menu. "We sold them for thirty cents. They were our Big Mac."

Today, John owns the Galardi Group, which includes Weldon's and Hamburger Stand restaurants in addition to Wienerschnitzel. (The "Der" was dropped in 1977. "It's too bad they changed the name," Glen says. "Kids liked it. They'd come up to the window and ask for 'der kraut dog, der mustard dog.'") Of 350 Wienerschnitzels nationwide, eighty are company-owned, and 270 are franchised; each averages annual gross sales of half a million dollars. John's first Der Wienerschnitzel continues to operate at Pacific Coast Highway at Gulf Avenue in Wilmington.

To avoid confusion with Taco-Tias owned by a former partner, Glen also needed to come up with a new name. When Bob Trujillo suggested "Taco Bell," Glen liked it.

"I'd been teased about my name when I was a kid—'ding-dong Bell,' that sort of thing. This gave the name a positive ring—no pun intended."

For the first Taco Bell, Glen picked a site in an incorporated city southeast of downtown Los Angeles. The location was in a growth area near a middle-class neighborhood, on a street with good traffic and numerous small businesses. But the lot was large.

Bob recalls, "It was at 7126 Firestone Boulevard, Downey. Glen would go there and walk up and down at four in the morning. I wondered if he was all there, the way he'd drink coffee and look around." Glen envisioned a village plaza, like those he and Bob had seen in Mexico. "Glen planned different little subleased shops that would sell tacos, cotton candy, and crafts, plus fire pits and mariachis. A place to sit, walk, eat, and be entertained."

Taco Bell archives

Downey, California, 1962. Glen opened the first Taco Bell at 7126 Firestone Boulevard.

Because Downey's sister city is Guadalajara, Mexico, Glen named the complex "Plaza Guadalajara." He hired an architect, Robert McKay, to design it, and paid for its construction with down payments from prospective tenants. In keeping with the Mexican theme, and because Glen felt a Taco Bell should look like a building that sold tacos, he asked Robert to give the new restaurant a south-of-the-border look.

The architect designed the tiny walk-up stand of stucco trimmed with brick. Archways framed a sheltered patio/order area, and the roofline incorporated a square bell tower. Robert recalls, "I told Glen the building would cost $7,000. Glen said he'd be happier with $4,000. With overages, it went to $8,500."

Roadwork threatened to put an end to his first Taco Bell, Glen recalls. "Right after we opened, the street was torn up. There was a deep trench along the front of the store." Yet in the evenings, he saw brake lights blaze as cars passed, then watched as "drivers went two blocks, turned around, threaded their way back through parking lots, then crossed a makeshift bridge to get to us. I'll never forget that line of headlights coming toward us."

Robert McKay also designed Der Wienerschnitzel's red-roofed A-frame eatery. "The idea was to create an inexpensive, easily recognized sign for the public. You let the building be the sign."

In June 1962, three months after he opened Plaza Guadalajara and the first Taco Bell, Glen registered Taco Bell as a California corporation owned by Glen and Martha Bell. Their four thousand dollars in capital equaled forty shares of stock, each worth a hundred dollars.

Over the next two years, he built eight more Taco Bells identical to the first.

Taco Bell archives

Marty recalls, "We moved often when Glen was building stores—Long Beach, Gardena, Altadena, and four places in Pasadena." But she was accustomed to a pack-and-move lifestyle; it was the way she and her parents had lived during the war. "You just accept it because you have to do it. We could throw all our stuff into two cars."

During the 1960s, the "Taco Bell boy" welcomed customers.

All profits went to developing the business, and money was tight. Marty remembers how Glen stayed awake three days and two nights in order to open a restaurant ahead of schedule, because every day of operation meant four hundred dollars profit: "Glen had built a store in L. A., and it was almost finished. The equipment was still in boxes, there was paper on the windows, the refrigerator wasn't stocked, and the fly fan wasn't connected. It passed inspection for fire safety, plumbing, and engineering. The health inspector was the last one. After he gives his approval, you can open. He came on Friday afternoon, and we thought he'd finish on Monday. But he must not have wanted to come back, because he gave us the go-ahead. We were shocked and delighted. But, of course, we were nowhere near ready to open. Glen rounded up employees from other stores and had them wash pans and clean windows. He got uniforms for new employees and called food suppliers. He worked through Friday night, all day Saturday, and Saturday night. Sunday afternoon we opened."

Taco Bell archives

Signs like this decorated construction sites of new Taco Bells.

A store's "grand opening" occurred after a restaurant had been open a few weeks and the manager and crew had attained optimum efficiency. Marty says, "We'd go over in the evening and park out in front—in those days, you parked right in front of the store, not alongside it—and sit on the fenders. Sometimes the kids were in their pajamas in the back of the car. Friends and suppliers would come by. It was fun, and it was our social life."

Bob Trujillo adds, "To attract attention, Glen would do something big. There were searchlights, mariachis, and free hats. You can imagine what people were thinking. They thought it was the World's Fair or something, and it was just this little taco stand. During one grand opening, my wife Phyllis and I drove by, and we couldn't believe it. There was Glen on the roof of the building, fixing balloons. He loved grand openings."

But such celebrations were expensive, and Glen's debts mounted.

"It was a struggle for him to pay me," says Macy Coffin, a building contractor. "Once, Glen gave me a pickup truck for putting in a store for him. Another time, he owed me three thousand dollars and told me, 'Macy, I don't have it.' I was used to it. He'd pay me so much a month. He was always honest and square."

John Galardi also used Macy's skills and resources. "John used to call me his dad. I mortgaged my house and loaned him thirty thousand dollars, and he built three hot dog stands with it."

Glen hired a friend of Bob Trujillo's, Paul Wesley, to oversee construction, install equipment, and maintain existing stores. Paul says, "I'll tell you one thing. Glen knows how to finagle his employees to work ten- and twelve-hour days. But it must not have been too bad, because they stayed with him."

In 1963, Glen leased office space in Palos Verdes Estates, a coastal community west of Long Beach, and hired a secretary and receptionist. Located near a golf course in a neighborhood of ranch-style homes and professional buildings, the Spanish-style office complex had an upscale ambience—precisely the image Glen wanted for Taco Bell.

"It was such a pleasant setting, and it had the feel of success," he recalls.

Glen also joined the Palos Verdes Rotary Club, and on a two-week Rotary Club tour to Toronto and New York, he met Jim Collins, who later founded Sizzler restaurants. At the time, Jim was in the hamburger drive-in business and owned the rights to Kentucky Fried Chicken in California.

Bob Trujillo and John Galardi also were aboard the Rotary Club's chartered jet, and the four men savored a rare opportunity to compare notes.

Glen says, "I had ten or fifteen stores and told Jim about tacos. John talked hot dogs."

Jim, like others in the burgeoning fast-food industry, aspired to be as successful as McDonald's. "Back when I got started, McDonald's was the only restaurant in the world doing a phenomenal business selling fifteen-cent hamburgers. I was building a coffee shop at the time and switched to a hamburger stand. I sliced potatoes, fried hamburger, and learned the business. I worked like a dog for thirty days. If I'd had the wisdom, I would have asked the McDonalds for the L. A. territory."

Coincidence also brought Glen into contact with the founder of another restaurant chain. As with Taco-Tia and El Taco, Glen used a commissary to service Taco Bell. Bob recalls, "It was on East Anaheim in Long Beach. I'd go there and visit Glen. One day he said, 'Come with me,' and we went around the corner, I think it was on Obispo, to a bakery."

"It had an old-fashioned screen door," Glen recalls. "They sold pies warm out of the oven all day long. My favorite was banana cream." The bakery was owned by Don Callender, son of Marie Callender.

Taco Bell's commissary, Glen adds, offered numerous benefits. Store managers didn't have to talk to salesmen or fill out purchase orders. Supplies arrived at, and were disbursed from, a central location. "Each manager called the commissary at midnight, after closing. We sent what they needed based on their volume."

Because the restaurants didn't include full kitchens, they were small and therefore inexpensive to build. Macy Coffin says early company-owned Taco Bells were "little bigger than garages"—about six hundred square feet.

Expensive equipment, including machines that grated cheese and shredded lettuce, were shared by all stores. The commissary system also reduced waste, ensured product uniformity and minimized in-store labor.

"Managers only had to train employees how to cook meat, fill taco shells, and take care of customers," Glen says. But because it added overhead, "the commissary was really a break-even thing, a service."

Yet a commissary system works well only if the stores it serves are in a limited geographical area. Because of Taco Bell's potential to expand into other regions, Glen realized future stores would have to be self-sufficient.

Circa 1964. Glen and Robert McKay worked with an architect in Palos Verdes to create the building that would become the standard for Taco Bells.

This meant the basic restaurant would have to be enlarged and redesigned to accommodate all aspects of food preparation.

Glen and Robert McKay worked with an architect in Palos Verdes to create a building that would become the standard for later Taco Bells. These were constructed of slump stone, a tan brick that resembles adobe.

Robert explains, "The building had to be a substantial architectural monument to put in the customer's mind that a good, substantial building equaled a good, substantial product. The building projected an image and was part of the educational process."

Above a red clay tile roof was a curved mission-style bell tower flanked with yellow letters within alternating blue and red squares. These spelled TACO BELL. Because each square was at a jaunty angle, "We called them 'tumbling blocks,' " Robert says.

On two sides of the building, protruding horizontally four feet below the roofline, were "outriggers"—Santa Fe-like logs that each held a wrought iron lantern. Above each outrigger was a sign that named one of the menu's five items: tacos, tostadas, burritos, frijoles, and chiliburgers (hamburgers made with taco meat, also called Bellburgers). Most Taco

Bells incorporated an outdoor eating area in front, surrounded by a low block wall.

Glen was proud of the restaurants' outdoor fire pits: waist-high rings of brick that contained porous rock and glowed with gas flames. "We were known for our bonfires. They created a really nice atmosphere, especially at night or when it rained." The fire pits later were discontinued due to a natural gas shortage.

Trash cans shaped like saguaro cactus were added later. They enhanced the building's design—so much so "we had to weight them to keep them from being stolen," Robert says. "We put a couple of cement blocks in the bottom of each can."

Glen watched each new Taco Bell like a racing fan who had bet on a horse. "That was the fun part," he says. "Every new location had its own potential. I didn't know what it was really worth until it opened." When a store did well, Glen adds, "I was as excited as if I'd found gold."

Only one, an existing stand Glen bought from a competitor, started out poorly. "It was doing sixty or seventy dollars in sales a day. I thought, if we're going to go broke, let's go broke doing some volume. We put all food items at fifteen cents, break-even. At the end of the year, we brought up the gross sales to ten thousand dollars a month." By then, Glen adds, the store had "the feel of success," and when he raised prices to nineteen cents per item, sales remained steady.

When Glen checked on restaurants, "I tried to get there at important times—noon, dinnertime, and late. There are so many things that go wrong late at night; that's when you see waste and stolen food. I always paid for my own items, even when the employees knew me. I tried to impress on the manager the importance of inventory control, and if anything was missing or stolen, we wanted to know about it."

He noticed if employees gave out too many napkins, or a handful of hot sauce containers instead of one or two. Glen also kept a set of scales in his car and could interpret how well a store was managed from a three-dollar order.

"A taco was supposed to weigh three ounces. It might weigh four or five, but I'd be really concerned if it was only two. Then profits were too good. The manager was shorting to make himself look better."

Glen's son Gary, who was eight at the time, recalls, "Dad had me trained. When we went to Taco Bells, I'd notice if the garbage cans had been emptied and whether the counter help was quick to ask, 'Can I help you?' He'd send me in, and then he'd watch through the window. I'd come back and report. We'd go to several Taco Bells in one evening."

Bob Trujillo's friend Bill Lindner adds, "Glen used to like to check on his stores at night, for research and development. But since he knew he'd be recognized, and they didn't know me, he asked me to go and bring him back sacks of Mexican food. So I'd go and buy a lot, maybe several dollars' worth. One time someone had put a tostada in a sack upside down. I thought it was funny, but Glen didn't. He was really upset."

Macy Coffin remembers how Glen caught a manager whom he suspected was dishonest. "Glen slipped a twenty-dollar bill into the store's floor safe. Sure enough, at the end of the day the guy didn't report he was twenty dollars over. He'd kept it."

Glen also checked on the competition, often accompanied by John Galardi. Macy recalls, "John, Glen, and I were eating lunch at a cafeteria in Long Beach, and they were talking about competing stands. I asked, 'How do you know what kind of business they're doing?' Glen said, 'John and I count tomato boxes and crates of lettuce, and talk to the delivery guy.' Glen knew from experience how many tacos and hamburgers they were making from how much meat and lettuce they used."

Glen adds, "John and I also figured out how well a competitor was doing by counting the number of employees. We figured one employee for every hundred dollars in sales per day. At the average fast-food stand, labor ran about 20 percent of gross."

When the stress became intense, Glen drove to Buena Park, northeast of Long Beach. His destination was a former boysenberry farm that owners Walter and Cordelia Knott had transformed into an Old West theme park.

"I used to go out to Knott's Berry Farm to sit and be by myself," Glen says. As he strolled through Ghost Town, Glen took pleasure in watching visitors experience various attractions, and envisioned how he might create his own theme park.

Glen lost track of time as he observed families peer into the watery-paned windows of buildings from old mining camps. He anticipated the startled screams of tourists when actors in period costumes staged a *High*

Noon shoot-out with flintlock guns that popped loudly and emitted sulfur-scented smoke. Late in the afternoon, he relaxed on a sun-warmed bench near a lacy Victorian depot and watched visitors board an 1880s passenger train.

If he was ever to accumulate the resources to create something comparable, Glen realized, he would have to expand his business beyond a handful of taco stands. The answer was to build a fast-food empire like McDonald's, which by then had grown to nearly seven hundred restaurants in forty-four states. And the only way to do that was to franchise.

The concept was beautifully simple: Glen would sell Taco Bell's name, trade secrets, and business format to independent owner/operators for an initial fee, plus ongoing royalties. This would give him a continuous supply of cash to expand and develop Taco Bell. In addition to Glen's hard-won business expertise, franchisees would benefit from joint advertising and combined purchasing power.

"There were a lot of reasons to go into franchising," Glen says. "I had gotten to the stage where I had everything right—the building, the food items, and the system. When President Johnson was elected, I bet on inflation. I figured we could risk money on ten-year leases because as prices of other items increased, the leases would stay the same yet gain in value."

In November 1964, Glen asked a young mortician, Wayne Milner, to join the staff as Taco Bell's first franchise salesman. Wayne says, "My wife was Bob Trujillo's secretary; that's how I met Glen. I was in my twenties and worked for my uncle, who owned a mortuary in Wilmington. I didn't know anything about the food business or about franchising. The whole idea was new. Glen convinced me I could do it."

Glen also realized Taco Bell's first franchisee had to be the right person, someone highly motivated and determined to succeed. Sales of additional franchises depended on it.

In early 1965, Wayne Milner sold the first Taco Bell franchise to a forty-three-year-old police officer with no restaurant experience and an unusual name: Kermitt Bekke.

Glen's Recipes for Success

#29: People who support your vision and take risks for you should share your success.

I needed money to expand my business, and when lenders turned me down, I went to my friends. I gave them generous terms because I wanted to show how much I appreciated their help. They understood what I was trying to achieve, and they deserved to be rewarded for taking risks on my behalf.

#30: Your building makes a statement about your business.

We wanted a Taco Bell to look like a building that not only sold Mexican food but also offered a substantial, quality product. Today, everyone knows about Taco Bell, so getting the point across with architecture is no longer necessary. What hasn't changed is what a restaurant's appearance says about its products and service. A clean, well-maintained store tells customers that employees have a good attitude, and the owner takes pride in the establishment.

#31: The heart of a business is people, not paperwork.

Taco Bell's growth was exciting but also incredibly demanding. I had to see to it that the same high standards I applied to my first store were met at ten stores. I was seldom in my office. I felt that sitting behind a desk doing paperwork wasn't as important as visiting stores, observing their operations, viewing new sites, and meeting prospective franchisees.

CHAPTER TEN

The First Franchise
1965

NO ONE CALLED THE BLUE-EYED OFFICER BY HIS FIRST NAME—he was "Becky" to friends and associates. Kermitt Bekke joined the Los Angeles Police Department in 1948. "I was shot once and beat up twice," he recalls.

Though he left the force thirty-five years ago, Bekke's soft voice retains a crisp politeness reminiscent of the TV series, *Dragnet*. Instead of "Pardon?" he says "Ma'am?" or "Sir?" and his whole body listens.

Bekke was born and raised on a farm in Minnesota. "Both me and Glen Bell were farm kids. We don't know when to stop working."

In 1964, the year the Beatles appeared on the *Ed Sullivan Show* and shocked the world with hair that hid their ears, Bekke was forty-two. He had served the citizens of L. A. for sixteen years, earned $1,100 a month, lived in Downey with his wife and two teenage sons, and had never opened a checking account. As a "juvenile investigator," Bekke spent his time following up on crimes committed by minors. "I knew Joe Zeller, one of the uniformed guys, who had a side job working for Glen, picking up money and banking it for Taco Bells. I didn't know what a taco looked like. I asked Zeller to let me ride with him."

In his methodical manner, the investigator observed the restaurants' operations. He found tacos tasty but liked the chiliburger even better. "I talked to a few Taco Bell managers. I thought it was an interesting business and got all the information I could. When I heard Glen Bell was thinking about franchising, I went to his office in Palos Verdes and waited for him." To pay the fifteen-thousand-dollar franchise fee, Bekke borrowed five thousand dollars from the Police Credit Union and obtained a ten-thousand-dollar second mortgage on his house.

Torrance, California, 1965. Kermitt Bekke, Taco Bell's first franchisee, surveys his nearly completed restaurant.

Bekke's fellow officers shook their heads when he told them he planned to buy a Taco Bell franchise. "A guy on the Police Department sat down with a pencil and a piece of paper and said, 'You've got to sell three or four tacos a minute.' And that was just to pay the rent. My dad said the same thing. Glen told me, 'When you open this up, you'll quit the Police Department.' I said, 'No way.' "

Glen picked the site for the store: a corner lot in Torrance, in the South Bay region of Los Angeles. It was an industrial area, but the intersection of Carson and Western was busy at all hours, even late at night.

"It was a working-class, blue-collar neighborhood," Bekke recalls. "Glen told me, 'In a low-income area, you can make more money than in a high-income area.' "

Bekke visited the owner of a McDonald's franchise down the street. "He was doing forty thousand dollars a month gross sales. I figured if I can do half or a third of that, I'm in tall cotton."

Glen adds, "A Taco Bell typically would do two-thirds the business of the nearest McDonald's. If they did fifteen thousand dollars, we did eleven thousand dollars."

Bekke's was the first Taco Bell designed to be self-sufficient. Unlike earlier company-owned stores, it was not dependent on a commissary. The eatery's larger size accommodated areas for the preparation of ingredients—lettuce, cheese, tortillas, meat, and beans—in addition to an assembly line for food orders.

Late one afternoon in April 1965, the new restaurant passed final inspection. Bekke recalls, "We decided to try it out, so we heated the stoves, and around seven or eight, we opened the order window. This guy came up to the window, handed me a dollar, and I said to Glen, 'Ohmigosh, do you have change?' We had to reach into our pockets. After an hour, we took in eighty-five dollars. Glen said, 'We've got a winner.'"

Bill Cason, who later franchised three Taco Bells in San Diego County, worked alongside Glen and Bekke that night. "It was a crazy scene," Bill says. "Everything started taking off. None of us had anticipated it. The location seemed to be quiet."

"That was without advertising," Bekke adds. "We had a two-week shakedown before the grand opening. It gave us time to train the crew. Glen sent employees and a manager over from other stores to show us what to do."

"We really didn't have to advertise," Glen recalls. "You could tell when you drove past, by the people lined up and the cars, that it was a success. Word got out."

But Glen went ahead with a lavish grand opening. It was an ideal opportunity to show prospective franchisees what Taco Bell had to offer. When he called searchlight companies, "One asked me how many I wanted. They had thirteen. I said, 'I'll take 'em all.' We had a couple on the Safeway lot next door and a couple across the street. They were all over the place. We lit up the South Bay."

Bekke adds, "The fire pit was going. We had a mariachi band, a car that tipped up to give kids rides, and straw hats with TACO BELL printed across the top."

"The scheduled grand opening was to last through Thursday and Friday," Bill Cason recalls.

"There was such a crowd, and Glen was having such a good time with the balloons, mariachis, and searchlights, that we extended it a day. We stayed open on Saturday until 2 in the morning. They were long days, too. We were bringing in close to three hundred dollars an hour, nineteen cents at a time."

On the second night, Bekke told Glen, "We've got a problem. The cash box we're using is so stuffed I have to stand on it to close it."

As employees filled taco shells and propelled them along the assembly line, they moved in sync, with the precision of a rowing crew. "We figured we were doing one taco every three seconds," Bekke says. "And we sold more than that because we were going so fast."

Bekke, however, had trouble with tacos. "I'd crush 'em in my hands and say, 'Aw, forget it.' I worked in the back room frying meat and making beans. We had seven employees at peak hours, one at each window and five on the line, and I was in the back frying meat, as fast as you could fry it, on two stoves."

Back in a mid-sixties Taco Bell, Bekke adds, "You made the food right in front of people. They could look in the windows and see everything. Glen liked it that way."

Tortillas arrived fresh every day from a tortilla factory. "One guy's job was to fry them in wire baskets and put the shells on racks. He did nothing else." Beans, Bekke says, "were forty-five minutes, start to finish, in the pressure cooker." He cooked twenty pounds at a time and mashed the cooked frijoles with a beater attached to a quarter-horsepower drill, "until the Health Department told me not to."

Taco sauce, processed at a factory according to Glen's specifications, came in gallon cans. Bekke recalls, "My mom and dad came to L. A. from Minnesota on vacation, and they wanted to help. So I gave them white hats and put them to work filling sauce cups, at a penny apiece. They'd line up the cups, pour in the sauce from the can, and snap on the lids."

The Torrance Taco Bell's first month's gross sales exceeded thirty-three thousand dollars. Bekke netted $10,053 profit. "It was almost ten times my salary." In less than two months, he recovered his initial investment.

Bekke remembers going to the bank. "I had eight thousand dollars in a briefcase. The gal asked me if I wanted to put some money into my new account. She suggested maybe a hundred or two hundred dollars. I opened the briefcase, and you should have seen her face. 'We'll have to count that in the back,' she said.

"I was wearing my work clothes when I went to the Cadillac dealer. One of the salesmen wouldn't wait on me; he didn't take me seriously. I bought a two-year-old blue Cadillac from another salesman, and I paid cash for it on the spot. The first salesman, boy, was he mad. He was kicking himself for missing out on the commission, but it served him right.

"I drove the Cadillac to the police station. That really got their attention. The Sheriff's Department, too." As Glen had predicted, Bekke quit the police force. He also bought a boat.

"I named it the *Taco Belle*."

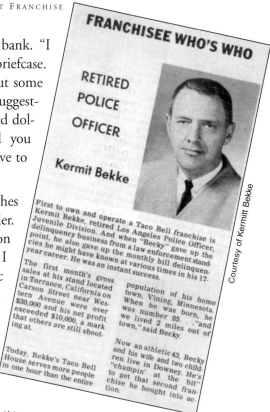

FRANCHISEE WHO'S WHO

RETIRED POLICE OFFICER

Kermit Bekke

Courtesy of Kermit Bekke

First to own and operate a Taco Bell franchise is Kermit Bekke, retired Los Angeles Police Officer. Juvenile Division. And when "Becky" gave up the delinquency business from a law enforcement stand-point, he also gave up the monthly bill delinquencies he might have known at various times in his 17-year career. He was an instant success.

The first month's gross sales at his stand located in Torrance, California on Carson Street near Western Avenue were over $30,000 and his net profit exceeded $10,000, a mark that others are still shooting at.

population of his home town, Vining, Minnesota. When he was born, he was number 85. . ."and we lived 2 miles out of town," said Becky.

Now an athletic 43, Becky and his wife and two children live in Downey. He's "champin'" at the bit" to get that second franchise he bought into action.

Today, Bekke's Taco Bell House serves more people in one hour than the entire

Bekke's phenomenal success helped sell Taco Bell franchises. From the second issue of the Taco Bell News.

"Bekke was a singer for Taco Bell," says Lou Novak, a former air force pilot who went to work for Glen as a franchise salesman the following month. "That's what it's called when a franchisee does so well he's telling everyone what a good deal he's got." Lou started with Glen at age twenty-five and has worked ever since in some aspect of franchising. "The key to a successful fast-food franchise is to make sure the first store is a winner. That first store, Bekke's, was the catalyst. And Glen gave his heart and soul to get the guy off the ground."

Glen adds, "It's funny the ideas people get. Some made remarks to me that implied, 'Don't you wish you'd opened that store instead of Bekke?' They thought I'd be jealous because I didn't own it. But I couldn't have hoped for anything better than what happened."

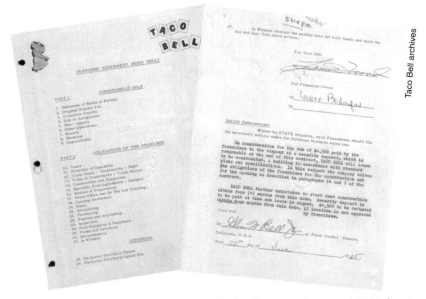

1965. An early Taco Bell franchise agreement. The franchisee agreed to pay a $4,500 deposit; Taco Bell agreed to start construction within four months.

Former L. A. police officer Wally Nissen was intrigued by an opportunity to own his own business and be his own boss. Wally, who visited Bekke's Taco Bell with fellow officer Abe Tavera, recalls that Bekke "ran up to three registers, got a fistful of money, assembled it into denominations and called Brink's (armored car service). He called Brink's three times a day." Both officers bought franchises.

Bekke introduced Abe to Glen. "Abe was a big guy, a motorcycle cop," Glen says. "The next time I saw him, he had three people lined up with their backs to him, their feet spread apart, and their hands flat against a fence. Abe opened a Taco Bell franchise in a rough neighborhood, but he could handle it."

Bekke remembers another friend of his: "He was up in Burbank, driving truck. He said, 'I'm scared. My back has been bothering me. What do you think? Should I buy a Taco Bell?' I told him, 'I can't make the decision for you, but I'll show you my books and give you all the information I've got. I'll let you be the judge.' He put his life savings into it, and he did real well. Ten or fifteen people I knew got involved, and a lot more I didn't know. I wanted them to be successful, and I wanted Glen Bell to succeed, too."

Bell family archives

Dancers at an early Taco Bell grand opening.

Today, Bekke is seventy-five and in excellent health, proud that he recently passed the flight physical to qualify for a pilot's license. He's as square-jawed and handsome as ever, with thick white hair, a tidy white mustache, and silver-rimmed glasses.

He has, however, two regrets concerning Taco Bell: "I figured I made a killing, so I sold the franchise after a year and a half. Also, I was going to climb up on the roof and ring the bell every day at noon, but I never got around to it."

Glen's Recipes for Success

#32: Pick people to help you expand your business who are as dedicated to it as you are.

Kermitt Bekke had a lot at stake in making his Taco Bell franchise work. He mortgaged his house and was eager to prove to his fellow police officers he'd made a smart move. Bekke was willing to put in long hours and do whatever was necessary to make the business succeed. He came to it with enthusiasm, energy, and a never-quit attitude. Bekke knew nothing about the restaurant business, yet he was an ideal franchisee.

#33: One good franchisee will attract others.

When Bekke's store took off, I was as happy as if I owned it myself. I couldn't have asked for anything better. I knew his success would attract others like him, and sure enough, several other L. A. police officers bought franchises. There was a strong camaraderie among them. Taco Bell supported them, and they supported each other.

#34: A founder's greatest reward is to see others benefit from what he started.

Since Taco Bell began in 1962, it has provided a good living for hundreds of franchisees and employees and has given thousands of young people their first jobs. We've also made a significant, positive impact on the American economy and provided a product of value to millions.

CHAPTER ELEVEN

Growing Pains
1965-1967

TACO BELL TOOK OFF LIKE A RUNAWAY HORSE—with Glen holding the reins.

Lou Novak recalls how easy it was to sell Taco Bell franchises: "I'd come back from lunch, and people would be waiting to see me. They'd mention Bekke's name. He'd briefed them already."

The company's success, however, was not guaranteed. In fact, Glen faced more problems than ever. "We had a hard time keeping up with the people who wanted to buy franchises. Also, existing franchisees wanted to expand their operations. With the pace we set, building one or two units a week, we didn't have the organization."

Glen adds, "In the beginning, I thought all we had to do was sell the idea, send someone to help them open, and get a check every month. We found out you've got to do a lot more to make sure a franchisee does well. There are supervising, correspondence, professional services, and more. If you don't provide them, you don't succeed."

Franchisees who had paid the fee and were waiting for a building often became impatient, for good reason: They had yet to receive any return on their investment. Of course, as Glen points out, if those same franchisees had built independent restaurants, they also would have waited months—and would have taken a greater risk.

In anticipation of a time when royalties would offset debts, Glen paid for current building costs with fees franchisees paid for future stores. "We put money in one big pot and disbursed it the best way we could. We were an honest company, with integrity. Otherwise we wouldn't have made it. The franchisees were dedicated to us, and we were dedicated to them. We put everything back in."

At the time, the practice of selling franchises was unregulated. A few rapidly growing companies were not as ethical as Taco Bell and funneled franchisee's fees into the pockets of unscrupulous owners. Laws passed since then vary in different states but are designed to protect the franchisee's investment. Typically, parent companies cannot spend a franchisee's fees as they please; the funds belong to the franchisee and must be used to provide land, a building, and other items specific to that franchisee's operation.

Advertisements in the Business Opportunities section of a typical mid-1960s *Los Angeles Times* included an average of thirty franchise opportunities, twenty food related. Today, of those restaurants, half no longer exist. Companies that took their franchisees' dreams down with them include Ozark Fried Chicken, Taco Lita, Dog House Coffee Shops, Ricky's Root Beer, and Twin Castle Restaurants. Survivors include A&W, Baskin-Robbins, Orange Julius, Denny's, International House of Pancakes, and Swensen's Ice Cream.

With such industry instability, it's surprising so few prospective Taco Bell franchisees asked to see a copy of the company's financial statement. If they had, they might not have risked their money. Landlords and lending institutions, on the other hand, remained cautious.

Because Taco Bell's balance sheet was heavy with liabilities, "At one time, I personally guaranteed $6 million worth of leases," Glen says. "I figured, if you go broke, you can only go so broke."

Glen also considered selling the company. Four years earlier, the McDonald brothers had sold their name and franchise rights to Ray Kroc for $2.7 million.

According to Bob Trujillo, "Glen still reminds me that he offered to sell me Taco Bell for one hundred thousand dollars. But back then, the company was in chaos. They were barely surviving. When you're building and growing fast, it's hard. There were a lot of problems. I admire Glen because he stuck with it."

Pomona, California, 1966.

Glen adds, "Most people don't believe you when you say you're not money hungry. I would have been satisfied to go at a slower pace. I could have gotten out, but I had employees and franchisees who were enthusiastic about the concept. If I'd sold out, I would have let them down."

Also, "I'd go by one of John Galardi's new Der Wienerschnitzels and think, 'I should be making the most of this taco business.' The old competitive urge would set in."

What caused Glen to lose sleep was not the threat of his own bankruptcy but the danger of taking others with him. "There were two brothers, young schoolteachers, who sold their house to pay for a franchise. When you see that, you want to make sure it goes."

Months later, when the teachers' Taco Bell opened in Santa Barbara, Glen chartered a Lear jet and flew company executives, employees, and prospective franchisees to the grand opening. "We wanted to show we were behind them 100 percent." After a record-breaking opening, the group from Los Angeles left late at night. "We looked down and located the Taco Bell by all the searchlights."

Thanks to Kermitt Bekke's police background, Taco Bell's first franchisee had impeccable credibility, but Glen cautioned eager new ones not to expect the same phenomenal success.

Lou Novak recalls, "We'd tell people, 'Bekke's is an exceptional store,' and they'd envision themselves making even greater profits than he did."

All franchisees had enthusiasm; few had restaurant experience. When it came time to close the deal with a barber, the man told Lou, "The money's downstairs. Come with me to get it."

Lou remembers the man's car was old and its back end low to the ground. "He opened the trunk, and it was full of bushel baskets of quarters—money he'd saved from tips. We carried it to Bank of America next door. It took them two days to count it."

The most in-demand area for franchises was the South Bay area of Los Angeles, near Bekke's store in Torrance. But as Taco Bells opened at the rate of two a week, they soon dotted the entire Los Angeles basin.

Glen's highest priority was the success of each new franchisee. "I'm not a flamboyant person, but I'm a big believer in advertising. A company store, when it opened, might do five thousand dollars a month, and with hard work, by the end of the year, ten thousand dollars. But if a franchise opened up and did only five thousand dollars, the franchisee would get discouraged and might not stick with it. A grand opening cost three thousand to four thousand dollars. We lost the first year's royalties, but it got the franchisee off to a good start. And that, in turn, helped the company. Franchises really sold by word-of-mouth. One person's excitement would sell someone else on the idea. We'd run an ad in the *L. A. Times* and get maybe two responses."

He recalls a grand opening at which a man told him he'd bought a franchise from another fast-food company. "They'd sent him a little packet worth ten dollars and told him, 'This is your grand opening.' He saw the mariachis and people by the hundreds and wished he'd bought a Taco Bell."

Glen's on-staff maintenance and construction supervisor, Paul Wesley, also sold franchises—inadvertently. "Potential franchisees would go and talk to him, and he'd sell more franchises than the salesmen," Glen says.

"People trusted him because he was working on the building." Franchisees bought a respected trade name and a business formula Glen had spent years perfecting, in addition to a turnkey restaurant. The fee, which soon increased to twenty-five thousand dollars plus 8 percent of the gross, provided training, assistance, and the right to use the company name.

During the first year, there was no formal school for franchise managers, and Glen hired them to work at existing Taco Bells. When their own stores opened, he worked alongside them.

"The building, equipment, signs, and lease (or mortgage) belonged to Taco Bell," Glen says. "That way we retained control."

Bob Trujillo, Glen's real estate consultant, accepted John Galardi's offer to become vice president of Der Wienerschnitzel. Bob later became president, and in 1981, retired. Today, Bob and his family own six Wienerschnitzels; his long-time friend and business partner, Bill Lindner, owns nine. Both also have made fortunes in commercial real estate.

Bob credits Glen for helping him get started: "He changed my world."

With Bob Trujillo no longer available, Glen asked one of Bob's former employees, Bruce Burrow, to scout sites. Bruce recalls the day he met Glen: "He had one of the first Ford Mustangs. It was baby blue. We gathered around it, and out unfolds this giant of a man."

Bruce and a friend who co-owned a stationery store, Hal Ezell, watched Glen fry tortillas at a Taco Bell. "We laughed. His hands were like hams. They were too big for the task."

Glen offered Bruce—and Hal, who became Bruce's partner—the choice of either a fee for finding store locations or a percentage of the stores' gross sales. Hal recalls, "In those days we needed money, so we went for the fee. But if we'd taken 1 percent of the gross for five years, with the volume those early stores generated, the amount would have been incredible."

Bruce remembers when Glen asked them to drive to San Diego to locate a franchise site. "I didn't know what a franchise was." (Today Bruce owns, among other commercial properties, the number-one producing Taco Bell in the nation, in Jonesboro, Arkansas; Hal became a Wienerschnitzel executive and a high-level government appointee.) With $150 from Glen to cover expenses, the young men headed south—and kept going.

"We went right on past San Diego to Tijuana," Bruce recalls. The Mexican border town was known for bars and nightclubs that stayed open all night. "Sunday afternoon, we knew we had to come back."

Because Glen suggested they look for "a corner lot with good traffic," Bruce and Hal selected the first one they saw with a "For Lease" sign. "We had no idea San Diego State University was on the hill, a half block away." As it turned out, "It was exactly the site Glen would have picked if he'd done it himself."

Glen spent months with Bruce and Hal as they scouted sites for Taco Bells throughout Southern California. Glen says, "You never saw two more aggressive guys. Bruce had ulcers at twenty-one, he went at it so hard. They'd get rooms at a hotel, set up four telephone lines, and call me the moment they found a location."

All three recall when Hal drove at top speed to the San Diego airport because Glen had a flight to catch. When they arrived, the plane was on the tarmac, propellers spinning. "Hal drove right up to it," Glen says. "But it was the wrong one." Bruce grabbed Glen's briefcase as Hal ran into the terminal, jumped over the airline counter and insisted employees locate and hold Glen's flight.

Bruce remembers Glen as "quite a guy. He was my hero at the time. One night, while we were scouting locations, we stopped at a motel. There weren't enough rooms, so Glen told us to take the beds. He slept on the floor. They don't make a finer guy than that. Also, he'd walk around the block to avoid a confrontation. He didn't want to hurt anyone's feelings."

Glen's trips to competing restaurants in other towns also are legendary. According to Bill Lindner, "Jack-in-the-Box had a new item Glen wanted us to try. One night around 11 P.M., he decided to drive us from L. A. to San Diego."

Taco Bell's first franchise salesman, Wayne Milner, adds, "Glen was a spontaneous guy. He'd say, 'Let's get something to eat.' I'd say, 'Where?' He'd say, 'San Francisco,' and we'd get on a plane."

Although Taco Bell demanded all his time and energy, Glen held onto his dreams. Wayne recalls Glen's comments whenever they saw a train: "He said he always wanted to own one. 'We'll build a track and charge people to ride it.' "

The franchise Bruce and Hal located near San Diego State University went to Wayne Milner's brother. Jim Milner, in his early twenties, had worked on a cattle ranch in the Imperial Valley, a desert area east of San Diego. His boss at the time, Larry Hahn, says the job had no future; the cattle business was going broke.

Larry helped Jim with the franchise fee. "We wanted him to get into something better than ranching."

After Jim's store opened, Larry recalls, "He would call us every night at 1 in the morning and tell us how much money was in the cash register, and how much he'd made that day."

After a few months, Jim bought a new Cadillac and drove to the town of Imperial. Larry recalls with a laugh, "All of us farmers were there with our dirty pickups and horses in trailers. We wanted to shoot him."

Soon after, Larry sold his ranch and also became a Taco Bell franchisee. "Many of the first Taco Bells were owned by people from the Imperial Valley. We handed out our profit and loss statements, and helped each other stay in business and succeed."

Larry's wife Val adds, "In 1965, we came in, and over the next two to three years, I counted—I made a list—Taco Bell sold 105 units to twenty franchisees from Imperial Valley."

Jim Milner and many other early Taco Bell franchisees who used profits to buy additional stores today are millionaires.

Lou Novak also did well; he recalls he made so much money from salary plus commissions he was embarrassed. "With 20 percent of franchise fees, I was making eight thousand to twelve thousand dollars a month."

Because of his air force background, Lou also was Taco Bell's company pilot. In August 1965, as he and Glen flew back to Los Angeles from San Diego in a small chartered plane, they saw columns of black smoke rising from an area north of Compton and east of Lynwood. Curious, they flew in for a closer look.

Glen recalls, "You could see flames and buildings on fire." After they landed, Lou discovered a bullet hole in one wing. Rioters in Watts had shot at their plane.

Not far from Taco Bell's office in Palos Verdes Estates, in Rolling Hills, Glen bought a ranch-style house in need of remodeling. He also put a down payment on a vacant lot with "an amazing ocean view." Fortunately, he didn't build on it.

Today Rolling Hills, though reputed to be the wealthiest incorporated town in America, also is known for ground slippage. In the northwest quadrant, topsoil sits on a foundation of slate. Pipes are above ground to avoid breakage when the ground slides, glacially, after heavy rains. Most homes built before the geological glitch was diagnosed have disintegrated, but a few determined residents cling to sunset-facing hillsides, their homes propped by adjustable jacks.

Bob Trujillo remembers when he and Glen, years later, visited the ocean-view lot: "It had a house on it, with a cable around it that tied it to a big pine tree."

In 1965, Glen bought a house in Rolling Hills on John's Canyon Road, a winding street that owes its bumps to tree roots rather than shifting sands. The lot was large, and Marty raised chickens.

"We also had four geese," Glen recalls. "We named them Lady Bird, Lyndon, Huntley, and Brinkley."

The home came with a bonus: a 1923 Rolls Royce valued at fifteen hundred dollars. "It'd be worth fifty thousand to sixty thousand dollars today. We ended up selling it for peanuts because we were putting every dollar into Taco Bell."

Her parents, Kathleen Bell recalls, didn't buy a color TV when the luxury item became available during the mid-sixties. "We weren't showered with a bunch of toys," she adds. "And we didn't eat junk food. Mom was a nutritionist. Ritz crackers were a treat, like cake. We ate whole-wheat bread. Taco Bell was OK, because corn and beans make a complete protein. But instead of soft drinks, Mom bought us milk."

Glen's mother Ruth, then sixty-three, lived with the Bells. Four years earlier, she had sold her Cedar Springs property to the California Department of Water Resources, which planned to flood the valley to create a reservoir (now known as Lake Silverwood).

Kathleen remembers her grandmother as hard working: "She prepared meals and then cleaned the kitchen and put everything away. Grandma Bell didn't sit down to relax until all the work was done. She'd start sewing in October to make all her Christmas gifts."

Rolling Hills, California, 1965. Glen with Taco the llama.

Rolling Hills, 1965. Kathleen and Gary Bell.

Kathleen was five when her father took her to a pet store and told her, "You can have anything here you want." She adds, "Keep in mind, my parents were conservative; we were not spoiled. My dad didn't normally do things like that. It was a child's dream."

The fragile-looking little girl first considered the snakes. "I was tempted, thinking about what Mom would say if I brought one home." Then, over the top of a fence, "I saw these fuzzy pointed ears, large brown eyes, long white eyelashes, and little llama lips."

The baby llama Glen bought his daughter was three-and-a-half feet tall. "I stood in the back of the Suburban and held it, with my arm around it," Kathleen says. "It licked my dad's neck and ears, and he laughed. The car window was down, and when we got home, the llama was looking out the window at my mom." They named it "Taco."

Scottsdale, Arizona, 1966. Grand opening of Taco Bell's first franchise outside California.

In the spring of 1966, Glen chartered an airplane and flew his wife, company executives, and prospective

Torrance, 1966. This fifteen-thousand-square-foot building housed Taco Bell's personnel and construction divisions as well as a training school for franchisees.

franchisees to the opening of Taco Bell's first out-of-state franchise in Scottsdale, Arizona. He also purchased a fifteen-thousand-square-foot building in Torrance to house personnel and construction divisions, as well as a new training school for franchisees. In the same building was Palos Verdes Supply Company, a wholesale restaurant supply warehouse owned and operated by Taco Bell.

As CEO of a fast-growing corporation, Glen became a public figure, and now-brittle news clips record his involvement in the local business community. One shows Glen presenting a check to a Boy Scout representative after a Taco Bell franchisee sponsored a promotion that raised $1,104.19. In another, Glen holds an award that honors him for "outstanding service furthering international understanding" between the United States and Mexico.

Glen served as chairman of the board of Lyric International, a nonprofit organization dedicated to promoting goodwill among nations through the arts. "They provided entertainment for our grand openings," he says. "We paid them a donation of fifteen hundred dollars a week." Lyric International had received an endorsement from President Eisenhower to develop a project that appealed to Glen's imagination: a cultural-arts park shared by the United States and Mexico. The governors of several border states were interested, Glen says, but the project eventually was canceled because of budget constraints.

San Francisco, 1966. Mariachis serenade visitors to Taco Bell's exhibit at a franchise exposition.

A June 1966 Taco Bell advertising brochure gives thumbnail sketches of twelve enthusiastic franchisees who had opened stores throughout Southern California. That same summer, Jingles the Clown presided over a grand opening in Norwalk; the business section of the *Los Angeles Times* listed eighty Taco Bells; Miss California 1964-65, Jeanne Venables, visited Taco Bell offices and nearby Marineland after hosting an opening in Sacramento; and mariachis serenaded Taco Bell's exhibit at a franchise exposition in San Francisco.

Los Angeles, 1966. Marty Bell, center, with beauty queens at a Taco Bell grand opening. Jeanne Venables, Miss California 1964-65, is at far left.

Soon after, Glen hired Robert McKay as head of real estate and construction. Robert recalls, "My job was to approve and develop sites, obtain permits, and all the steps of developing Taco Bells."

Paperwork never gathered dust on Robert's desk; the architect was organized and attuned to detail. His interest in the company "evolved as a result of conversations Glen and I had, often at building sites. Most architects tend to be artistic and creative rather than business-oriented. I've always had an intense interest in business."

Robert adds, "When I closed my office and went with Taco Bell, Glen was honest with me: 'I can't pay you.' I was married and had a small son. Yet I was convinced Taco Bell was worth the gamble because of the uniqueness of the product in an emerging fast-food market. I saw there was a niche for it, and I believed in it. I went to my wife and told her that after twelve years as an architect, I wanted to quit the profession and live off our savings. I give her a lot of credit for supporting me in this decision. I worked without a salary for six months. It was understood between us that Glen would make it worth my while. I trusted Glen, and he came through. We cut a deal for 15 percent of the company."

Robert, who stayed with Taco Bell until the early eighties, says he often has thought of how he went to work for Taco Bell for nothing. "It's important to believe in the company you work for. In a hiring situation, I would interview a person who was qualified, and then the talk would get around to salary. I'd say, 'This position pays twenty-five thousand dollars a year.' They might say, 'I have to have at least thirty thousand dollars.' I would then offer twenty-five thousand with substantial stock options, and they would refuse. Thinking back on it, because of the way the company (and the value of the stock) grew, that was probably the most expensive five thousand dollars that person ever turned down."

An early 1967 photo of Taco Bell's administrative and sales personnel, in a conference room at the Torrance office, shows Glen, Robert, and fourteen other men. All wear business suits and are seated around a long table. Typical topics of discussion at such meetings included the qualifications of possible new employees and franchisees and how franchise salesmen might be more effective.

Glen says, "I encouraged them to attend grand openings and to bring prospective franchisees with them."

The men also debated methods to boost sales volume. Glen believed one way was for Taco Bells to stay open until 11 P.M.—even though most restaurants closed at 9 P.M. "It may not seem like you're doing much

Torrance, 1967, Taco Bell administrative meeting. Glen is seated at the head of the table; Robert McKay is on his left. Wayne Milner (corner, standing) is holding a drink cup. Lou Novak is on his left, standing.

business, but the sales you do make are important. Because other places are closed, you get their customers. You might think a new customer is only worth whatever profit you make on a sale. But I put a much higher value on him, because he'll come back—and he'll spread the word to others about Taco Bell."

Franchisees' concerns were given priority, Glen adds. "We talked about ways to speed up our real estate acquisitions. If there was no way to do that, we sometimes hired the franchisee." For example, Reynolds Jensen, who later franchised a dozen prosperous Taco Bells in Fresno, started out as a field (restaurant openings) supervisor. "It took care of his need and also one of ours."

Occasionally, however, franchisees tried to take advantage of the company. One couple with a store in Garden Grove said their business had been hurt by road construction, and asked Taco Bell management to reduce their rent and other fees they owed.

Glen recalls, "We did. Later, at the end of the year, we read their financial statement and found out they'd made twenty-five thousand dollars— which was more than our top managers were making at the time."

Glen had little respite from business. He remembers a Christmas party for the employees and franchisees of both Taco Bell and Der Wienerschnitzel held at John Galardi's home. "One franchisee wanted to know when I was going to get his store done. An employee's wife asked when I was going to give her husband a raise. Even the maintenance man talked about how he needed a new pickup. John and I, Bob Trujillo, and a few others ended up in the bathroom together. We still laugh about it. It was the only place we could go to get away from people who wanted something."

Glen found it difficult to be firm with franchisees or to fire anyone who, though well-intentioned, performed below par. Robert McKay easily dealt with these and other issues and soon became Glen's most valuable employee.

Robert recalls, "Glen and I would stand in the parking lot kicking gravel and talking until three or four in the morning. We'd start out discussing our dreams and aspirations for the company and for the concept of Mexican fast food. I'd ask Glen's help understanding the ins and outs of the food business. With an architectural background, I had a lot to learn.

"Sometimes we'd go and visit a store or two or sit and drink coffee. The topic we discussed last, because Glen found it the least interesting, was setting up the administration of the company. Glen is an entrepreneur and a creative genius, but he's not much of an administrator. He didn't have a vice president or CFO (chief financial officer), so he pretty much ran things by the seat of the pants. Every company starts out disorganized, and Taco Bell was no exception."

Even though Robert often didn't get home until dawn, "I was in the office the next day by 8 A.M. When the excitement of a venture is that great, the adrenaline keeps you going."

Glen also appreciated Robert's initiative. "When we'd have a meeting, the average employee would say, 'We got problems with this and this, and what are you going to do about it, Mr. Bell?' McKay would come up with a problem and say, 'This is how I think we can solve it.' I had a lot of confidence in his judgment. I would go off and want to buy a piece of

Anaheim, 1967. Taco Bell's one hundredth store opened at 400 South Brookhurst.

property for a Taco Bell, and McKay was always very careful not to overstep on the transaction."

Glen promoted Robert to vice president of administration. Soon, however, grand openings caused friction between them.

"For a shy person, Glen had a theatrical bent," Robert recalls. "He'd be right in the middle of things at a grand opening. In the early days, I told him we couldn't spend five thousand dollars on a grand opening because we didn't have it. Glen said the grand opening was so important, it had to happen. I didn't disagree about the importance. I wanted to stay within the limits of what we could afford. I tried to keep Glen's entrepreneurial energies going without bouncing checks, and the grand openings were breaking us. Glen would call the searchlight company, ask them how many we'd ordered, and change it from four to eight.

"Some of those grand openings came at a high price. I'd think, 'My gosh, we can't even meet payroll.' I was spending a couple of hours every day with creditors. I'd tell them, 'Trust us, we'll pay you.' Most were patient, and everyone eventually got paid."

Taco Bell's one hundredth store opened in Anaheim, at 400 South Brookhurst, in January 1967. An advertising flier promised "contests,

Taco Bell archives

Anaheim, 1967. Hot air balloon operator with Glen, center, and Robert McKay.

clowns, dancers, dignitaries, and a hot air balloon the size of a house floating above the picturesque adobe restaurant . . . Miss California 1966-67, Sue Bradley, will reign over the Ciento Celebration, which also features the famed Taco Bell Mariachi band." A photo taken during the event shows three men in the basket of the hot air balloon: a grinning Glen, a sanguine-looking Robert, and a pipe-smoking balloon attendant wearing a serape and sombrero.

In May, Glen left on a business trip to scout sites for Taco Bell's proposed expansion into the southeastern United States.

Marty recalls a phone conversation: "Glen said, 'Hi, have you been to Florida?' Of course, I'd lived in Tampa with no air-conditioning during the war. The humidity was so bad, we had to keep our shoes in the water closet, because the leather would mildew. Glen asked, 'Do you want to come and stay for a while?' I had just bought some really nice furniture, on credit, for the house in Rolling Hills. Besides, summer was when everyone *left* Florida. Glen didn't tell me he had put a down payment on a three-bedroom, two-bath home for us in St. Petersburg."

Glen's Recipes for Success

#35: Never take advantage of others—even if it's legal.

Franchising was so new in the early sixties that it was unregulated. We could have taken the franchisees' fees and used them for things that had nothing to do with building stores or helping them get started. It wasn't against the law, and other companies did just that. I'm proud that Taco Bell was—and still is—an honest company dedicated to its own long-term success and that of its franchisees and employees.

#36: Control your growth, or it will control you.

We reached a point at which Taco Bell had grown beyond what I had anticipated, or even wanted. The only way we could stay solvent was to continue to grow. At times the stress was so intense, I was tempted to sell. I stayed because people were counting on me. I didn't want to hurt them or the business we all had worked so hard to build.

#37: Challenge employees to recognize problems. Reward employees who generate solutions.

The more Taco Bell grew, the more I depended on my employees. People who looked beyond problems and found solutions were quickly promoted. I wasn't as concerned with their education or backgrounds as I was with their attitude. I looked for people who understood where we were headed, were eager to learn, and who made Taco Bell their priority.

Glen's Recipes for Success

#38: Employees' enthusiasm is essential to success.

There's an intensity about beginnings that is demanding, yet very rewarding. Taco Bell is experiencing this once again with the founding of Tricon Global Restaurants. To propel a venture forward, you have to invest in good people, trust them, and encourage them to voice their ideas. When they know they're being listened to and are part of a dynamic team, they come to work excited and share a vital determination to succeed.

CHAPTER TWELVE

Tacos in Texas
1967-1969

THE FRANCHISEE WAS POLITE BUT INSISTENT. "Mr. McKay, I'm sure you're good at your job, but if it's all the same to you, I'd rather talk to Glen Bell."

Glen recalls, "For the first hundred stores, I worked closely with the franchisees, and it went well. But when we got up to 150, I didn't have time to help people individually." Yet many franchisees refused to discuss their concerns with anyone else.

He decided Taco Bell needed to hire a people-oriented person who knew the fast-food business, a man of integrity who understood how franchisees depend on good management.

"If a company makes bad decisions, a franchisee has no choice but to go along with it," Glen says. Early franchisees who worked with John Gorman, who was hired by Glen and Robert McKay as director of operations, today speak of him with admiration.

"John's a problem solver, a peacemaker," says former franchisee Larry Hahn. "Glen's brilliant at putting ideas together, but John kept in direct contact with us guys who were having a tough time."

Robert adds, "John has a tremendous way with people. Even if he had to tell them something distasteful, the franchisees loved him."

Today, as then, John Gorman is a tall, slender man with impeccable manners, a direct gaze, and a grin that puts others at ease. After he graduated from San Diego State University in the mid-1950s, he worked for an innovative new company in the same city: Jack-in-the-Box, a restaurant chain known for its hamburgers, happy-face clown, and drive-through service.

John managed Jack-in-the-Box as the company grew to include one hundred restaurants in the Southwest. He left when Ralston Purina took over in 1965. "I didn't want to work for a large company."

He was familiar with tacos. In fact, he had introduced them to Jack-in-the-Box. "My first experience with the taco was when I heard about a guy selling them in San Bernardino. I went up there, and Glen showed me around. I brought the fast-food taco back to San Diego." (John explains Jack-in-the-Box made tacos differently: "Because we had to cook them in a fryer, they were preformed, and the meat filling and tortilla were cooked at the same time.")

John describes Taco Bell's financial situation in the mid-sixties: "They had to make changes. They were about to go broke." Glen, he adds, had hired "a number of good people," and John offered guidance based on what had worked well at Jack-in-the-Box.

When it came to the design of the restaurant itself, John suggested only minor revisions. "Glen had a very sound, efficient operation. From taking orders to handing the customer the food, the whole thing flowed great. We could do low or high volume and still be efficient." Unlike a McDonald's or Burger King, "the system worked as well with two as it did with six people, so the number of employees could be adjusted according to customer demand."

Glen, John adds, "was a genius, the way he developed those five food items: the taco, burrito, tostada, frijoles, and chiliburger. All combined one or more basic ingredients—tortilla, meat, beans, cheese, lettuce—and all were priced the same."

Franchisees outside Southern California, however, confronted a clientele who had never tasted Mexican food. John recalls, "Our greatest challenge was to educate people."

John says Glen also shared an important similarity with Jack-in-the-Box founder Robert O. Peterson: "They didn't interfere with their management team. Glen knew what he did well. What he didn't do well, he stayed out of."

John remembers Glen's schedule: "He'd come in at noon or 1 and work through the night. A meeting would last until midnight; then Glen would say, 'Let's go down to the Farmer's Market in L. A.' It was open twenty-four hours. He loved to see people buying produce and food. He'd stand by the turnstiles, sometimes two and three hours at a time. He watched to see if they looked happy and what they were buying. We'd drive from Torrance to downtown L. A. and get home at 4 A.M. or 5 A.M. After one or two trips to the Farmer's Market, I tried to duck out of it."

Glen says, "We were so busy putting out fires and running the company, at the speed we had to go to keep building, when it came 5, you finally had time to sit and talk. By 9, half the employees would go; half would stay another hour. By 11, there'd be four or five of us, then just Gorman, McKay, and me."

Much of the time, the three discussed Taco Bell's financial concerns. Franchises were selling well, and business was good at established stores, but dozens of others, either newly opened or under construction, had yet to pay for themselves.

"Every emerging company is a risk," Robert says. "We needed capital to keep growing. I went to one bank that asked me for a pink slip on a car for collateral. I knew I was at the wrong bank. I went to Union Bank in the South Bay and talked to Jack Heidt, the manager, and he took a look at our books and records. He said, 'You're not a bankable company, but I'm impressed by what you've accomplished. Let me run some numbers.' Two days later, his bank gave Taco Bell a three-hundred-thousand–dollar loan. They took us on faith."

Taco Bell management also decided that franchise salesmen should be salaried rather than on commission. Glen recalls, "We had trouble with them making promises that the company didn't want to keep. For example, they'd give a franchisee an option to buy a second store as a part of the deal, and we preferred to wait and see how well the franchisee did with the first. Or they'd sell a twenty-five-thousand-dollar franchise for a five-thousand-dollar down payment."

With Glen's approval, John and Robert reorganized Taco Bell's staff and formalized the location criteria for new stores. According to John, a site had to have good visibility, easy access, and street traffic of more than fifteen thousand cars a day. "There had to be a population of twenty-five thousand people within a mile radius, middle to lower income, families and young people. Because of the price of the items, nineteen cents, we aimed at the blue-collar worker."

In mid-1967, Glen appointed Robert the company president; John, vice president. Glen retained the titles of CEO and chairman of the board.

Among the directors was John Kilpatrick, a build-to-suit investor who owned the land and buildings of many early Taco Bells. He recalls, "Glen had an excellent concept. I didn't know him well, but I respected him. Gorman was the hardest-working man I've ever seen. He was the right guy at the right time. McKay was a conscientious, no-nonsense guy, perfect in what he was doing. I thought they made a wonderful team."

"I feel that's where I did a good job," Glen says. "I was able to attract good people to do what I couldn't do. I'm still grateful to them. People like myself who start things are not necessarily the ones who continue to run them."

Glen began to focus his creative and entrepreneurial energies on Taco Bell's eastern expansion. When he opened a regional office in Florida in the summer of 1967, his goal was to persuade an untried market to buy an unfamiliar product. At the same time, John Gorman learned it was possible for a market to be *too* familiar with tacos.

According to former franchisee Larry Hahn, "We didn't realize selling tacos in West Texas was like selling ice cream to Eskimos. They sold tacos on every street corner and even in drug stores. The customers had an idea how tacos should taste, and Taco Bell wasn't it."

John had persuaded Larry and his wife, Val, to exchange their San Diego store for a new one in El Paso, a city at the western tip of West Texas. The Hahns were ideal pioneers: young (early thirties), energetic, and enthusiastic about Taco Bell. El Paso, like their hometown of Imperial, was a border town with a hot, dry climate. Unlike San Diego, it would be their exclusive territory.

Even so, when Larry asked his petite, hard-working wife, "Hey, babe, how'd you like to move to El Paso?" Val responded, "You've *got* to be kidding."

Val recalls, "The location of the first store in El Paso had been picked out for us. When we arrived, we found out the builder had run out of money and hadn't finished the building. We were in a hurry. We had to open in fifteen days because we needed the income. We gave the builder all we had, $3,500, which was the money we got from selling our house. We stayed in a beat-up hotel across from the building site, and let the manager think Larry was rich, Mr. Taco Bell himself, because we needed to stay there on credit. We didn't tell him all we had were three hungry kids, a poodle, and an old pickup truck."

As the store neared completion, vandals pushed bottles into the walls (the plaster was soft) and dumped paint on the floors. "We

El Paso, Texas, 1968. Franchisees Larry and Val Hahn.

had to clean it all up," Val says. "We come from a ranching background, so we were used to working from 4 in the morning to dusk. By the time we opened, we were down to our last twenty-five dollars."

But they soon discovered El Paso's predominately Hispanic population "wasn't interested in tacos from California," Larry says. "They had their own way of making them." As sales limped along, Larry took a second job and attempted to sell the franchise. "We ran an ad in the *Wall Street Journal* and didn't get a single response. We had no choice; we had to stay in business."

He adds they didn't blame Taco Bell. "You couldn't get too mad at the company. We were all struggling together."

John Gorman flew to El Paso, evaluated the situation, and reduced their rent and royalties. Even so, the Hahns' situation became desperate. When they could no longer pay their rent, Larry says John told them, "I want you to take the first fifteen hundred dollars of the gross that goes into the register and use it to feed your kids."

"We tried not to act surprised," Val recalls. "We didn't tell him we only needed $350. That was all we ever drew in a month. Our kids would eat tacos and burritos hot or cold."

With the support of Taco Bell's management, the Hahns became creative. Because customers complained the sauce was too mild, Val drove across the border to Juarez and bought gallon containers of *jalapeño* chiles. "I ground them up in a blender. They were so strong the acid wore away the blades and burned my hands. Our kids filled thousands of little cups (with snap-on lids) with jalapeño sauce."

They also advertised on television. "We probably were the first Taco Bell franchisees to do TV ads," Larry says. "We sponsored Bozo the Clown, an afternoon kids' show. The local station wanted to get Bozo started and didn't charge us anything. We threw the ads together on a shoestring."

Val adds, "Because it was a kids' show, we decided to offer a free taco to any child who came between three and four on a particular day. When you give something away in El Paso, they really turn out. Around two thousand came. We had kids jammed up against the counter so tight they couldn't move."

The Hahns eventually developed a clientele and built fifteen Taco Bells in the El Paso area. Today, the retired multimillionaires own homes in New Mexico and California, a private plane, a deluxe motorhome, and a yacht (the *Valentina*).

Larry says, "Young people ask me, 'How can I do what you did?' I tell them, 'Sell your house and everything you own, uproot your family, move to a remote town, and work seven days a week.' When they hear that, they lose interest."

Taco Bell's success in Florida depended on Glen. The Hahns' experience proved every new region was a gamble, and Southerners, Glen discovered, had strong opinions concerning food. At a restaurant in northwestern Florida, a waitress told him, "I'm so sorry. We're out of grits." Glen recalls, "I couldn't have cared less. Then the manager came out and apologized."

Grandma Bell remained in Rolling Hills while Marty and the children moved to Florida for the summer—and soon wished they could stay longer. Though their visit coincided with the hottest time of the year, Gary, ten at the time, says it didn't matter. "We were in the water as much as out."

Their St. Petersburg home was on a "finger," one of many man-made strips of land that extend into the bay and waterways. Housing developers, Marty explains, "dredged white sugar sand to form a peninsula, built a sea wall around it, put a paved street down the middle to make a cul-de-sac, and built homes around the perimeter. Each house had its own boat dock."

Glen's salary at the time was $3,500 a month. The mortgage payment on the three-bedroom, 1,500-square-foot house was $160 a month. None of the children he played with, Gary says, nor their parents, had heard of Taco Bell or eaten Mexican food. "There were no Mexicans there like there were in the Southwest."

Just as Marty remembered, Florida's air was heavy with moisture. "Fortunately, the house was refrigerated. The air-conditioning went out only once, during a lightning storm." The neighborhood was wonderful, she adds. "It was easy to get acquainted. There were a lot of little kids and even ladies who wanted to play bridge." Many of the husbands were stationed at a nearby air force base. "Air force people are gregarious. They know you're new and need friends. We looked out for each other's children. It was a nice community."

Kathleen recalls, "We played in the street, and people would sit in their front yards. There'd be a watermelon floating in the pool. It was a real neighborhood, with ball games in the cul-de-sac, tag, and hide-and-go-seek." She was six at the time and listened intently as grown-ups spoke of going to a special place they called "*My ami.*" The little girl looked forward to a time when she could have her own "*ami.*" "It was a place older people went to, to have fun and relax. I thought maybe it was provided by the government."

Marty remembers St. Petersburg as an ongoing adventure. "We had a power boat, the *Little Joe II*, and went all over. We'd explore the waterways, and the sea life was amazing. We went to Bird Key to collect shells." They also enjoyed snorkeling and water skiing.

As summer ended and it was time for the children to start school, Marty decided the family would remain with Glen in Florida. He arranged to sell their home in California (the llama went with it) and found a house for Grandma Bell not far from theirs.

Courtesy of Deloris Lukens

St. Petersburg, Florida, circa 1969. Glen's mother, Ruth Bell.

Marty recalls, "Ruth loved the pool at her house. She'd have a friend come over, and they'd go swimming. I'd go there, and they'd be in the water, hanging onto the side."

Deloris and Dorothy, two of Glen's sisters, came to visit. According to Gary, "They took Grandma Bell for a little trip across the state to Daytona, but they got caught in a Florida rainstorm, and it scared them half to death."

From his office on Thirty-fourth Street in St. Petersburg, Glen maintained daily contact with Taco Bell's main office in California. "He'd call and we'd talk for hours," Robert recalls.

As Florida's first Taco Bell took shape at Thirty-fourth and Fifth, Glen hired a manager, planned a grand opening, and contacted local newspapers.

Paid advertisements heralded the store's November 29 opening, listed the menu, and defined each item. Within the new restaurant were large color photos of the five menu items above written descriptions of their ingredients and phonetic pronunciations of their names.

Taco Bell archives

St. Petersburg, 1967. Glen and Marty in the St. Petersburg Times.

In regions unfamiliar with Mexican food, Robert explains, "Customers would order a '*take-oh*' instead of a '*tah-co*,' a '*toast-ay-doh*,' instead of a '*tost-ah-dah*,' or '*free-joe-lees*' instead of '*fri-hoh-les*.' "

Two weeks after Florida's first Taco Bell opened with a lavish, mariachi-serenaded event, an interview with Glen and Marty ran in the *St. Petersburg Times*. The photo that accompanied the article shows the smiling couple seated at their kitchen table, assembling tacos and burritos from bowls of lettuce, meat, and cheese. Glen wears a large, elaborately embroidered black sombrero. The article describes the new restaurant, introduces the Taco Bell chain, and gives recipes for the "Bell family's favorite foods." These include "Guacamole Sauce," "Mexican Pinto Beans," and, perhaps because Marty spent much of her childhood in the South, "Pralines."

The reporter defined a tortilla as "a thin pancake which serves as a base (much like a bun) for various Mexican dishes," a "tostado" as "a tortilla pancake served topped with frijoles or beans."

Taco Bell archives

Lakeland, Florida, 1968.

Glen opened Florida's second Taco Bell in Lakeland in April 1968. According to the caption of a news photo, the city's mayor "toasted the event's future success with a refreshing drink of Florida orange juice!"

Glen credits the accountant at the Florida regional office for suggesting a use for the "Taco Bell boy," a seven-foot-tall fiberglass sculpture of a smiling Hispanic wearing a serape and sombrero. When they secured it to water skis and towed it through St. Petersburg's inland waterways, "It stopped traffic," Glen recalls. "It was a great publicity stunt."

In June, Taco Bell's St. Petersburg store manager thanked his customers, in a newspaper ad, for consuming "300,000 tacos, 63,000 burritos, 46,000 tostadas, 78,000 chiliburgers, and 12,000 frijoles" since December. The ad includes a description of tacos: "Those delicious crunchy crisp tortillas filled with juicy all-lean beef, cheddar cheese, crisp lettuce, and our delicious Taco Bell sauce." In August, Glen escorted a shy brunette beauty queen, Miss Mexico, to the opening of Taco Bell's 270th restaurant in Springfield, Ohio.

St. Petersburg, 1968. Glen (in his backyard) gets ready to secure Taco Bell's mascot to water skis.

Early the following year, John Gorman offered Harry Buseman, a franchisee who owned Taco Bells in Ventura and Oxnard (California), the exclusive right to expand the chain throughout Florida.

"My hobby is sailing," Harry says with a smile. "Everyone has his price." Harry's risk was considerably less than the Hahns' because Taco Bell management had learned the hazards of sending franchisees into unproven territory.

Harry saw Glen several times a week at Taco Bell's St. Petersburg office. "We'd discuss expansion, growth, and menu items." Harry also accompanied Glen on eating excursions. "He liked to check on other fast feeders. He'd sample a little bit of everything. It was hell to keep up with him. He'd consume all this food and expect everyone else to do it, too."

Because it was difficult for Taco Bell's California headquarters to buy in bulk and provide discounted items to stores in Florida, Harry set up his own distribution system. "I bought a meat plant and a paper company and

Springfield, Ohio, 1968. Glen with beauty queens at the opening of Taco Bell's 270th restaurant.

1968. Glen and Miss Mexico.

bought directly from manufacturers. It was learn-as-you-go. Glen's input really helped."

Over the next two decades, Harry became Taco Bell's largest franchisee. "I had twenty-six stores in five Florida counties." Now retired, the St. Petersburg resident cruises the Caribbean and Atlantic seaboard in his seventy-three-foot motor yacht.

Also in 1969, as royalties from established franchises plumped the company's bank accounts, Taco Bell at last attained financial stability. In the fall, six weeks before Glen's forty-sixth birthday, Taco Bell had its first public stock offering.

Seven years earlier, with four thousand dollars, Glen had incorporated Taco Bell with forty shares valued at one hundred dollars each. When the company offered its stock to public ownership on October 21, 1969, "it underwent a thirty-thousand-to-one split," Glen says. Underwriters set the market price per share at eleven dollars. Although he sold 125,000 shares, Glen was still the principal stockholder. The second largest was Taco Bell president Robert McKay.

"The primary purpose of the stock offering was for the company to acquire operating capital," Robert explains. "Glen put some shares with it so he could have cash. From Glen's standpoint and mine, as primary shareholders, the public offering was an exciting and significant event. It established the company's value. For the first time, we knew how much our equity in Taco Bell was worth."

When Taco Bell "went public," Glen sold a fraction of his ownership and received a check for slightly more than $1 million. The cash had no strings attached. He could spend the money as he pleased.

Glen's Recipes for Success

#39: Be generous and open.

People become franchisees because they want the security of a proven business formula and the ongoing support of the parent company. The downside is that franchisees can't control corporate decisions that impact their livelihood. It's tempting for a company to take advantage of franchisees and to ignore them. Yet because franchisees, managers, and employees come into contact with customers, their enthusiasm and input are essential.

#40: Find people who know things you don't.

I enjoyed conceptualizing the business, getting it started, and watching its positive impact on customers, employees, and franchisees. But I'm an entrepreneur, not an administrator. Taco Bell prospered because I recognized my limitations, hired professional managers to make up for them, and knew when to let go.

#41: Attracting good employees is a skill in itself.

Employees see their bosses as role models. If you're dedicated to the business, willing to work hard, are honest and reliable, and treat others with courtesy and respect, you'll encourage those attributes in those who work for you. They, in turn, will expect and reinforce the same qualities among themselves.

#42: Develop a "never quit" attitude.

Larry and Val Hahn's Taco Bell franchise succeeded against enormous odds because they were focused, committed, and determined. They listened to their customers, made necessary changes, and never missed an opportunity to promote their business. They worked long hours and did without luxuries in order to meet their long-term goals.

CHAPTER THIRTEEN

Florida
1969-1974

AS A MILLIONAIRE, GLEN COULD HAVE JUST ABOUT ANY-THING. His dilemma, if it can be called that, was to decide what he wanted. He also had the potential to be much wealthier, should he decide to liquidate more Taco Bell stock.

Glen remembers what it was like to receive a million-dollar check: "You expect everything to change, but nothing does, not right away."

Marty, her son recalls, continued to drive "a brown Ford Galaxie 500 they'd bought for two hundred dollars." She was as thrifty as ever, Gary says, and was years ahead of her time when it came to recycling used items. "We never threw anything away. Mom used to throw coffee grounds under the gardenia bush."

Kathleen says the most significant benefit of wealth for her parents was relief from worry. Marty agrees. "In a new business you're always concerned about paying the bills."

Glen decided to have some fun with the million-dollar check. He took it to a small bank near Taco Bell's office in St. Petersburg, deposited it, and waited for it to cause a flurry among bank personnel.

"I thought the president might at least invite me in for a cup of coffee," Glen recalls. But the only response, days later, was a phone call to ask how he wanted the funds handled.

He decided to hire a secretary to help him keep track of his personal finances and asked Taco Bell's accounting firm to evaluate candidates. The company recommended Ruth Bradley.

In an accent that might have come over on the *Mayflower*, the former Bostonian says she moved to Florida in 1969 because "I had all I needed of snow." She adds, "I didn't know what a taco was. No one in New England ate them then." Glen addressed his diminutive, fiftyish secretary as "Miss Bradley;" she called him "Mr. Bell." After Miss Bradley settled into Glen's office, she discovered "He's not a nine-to-five person. Mr. Bell came in when he felt the need to. I got used to that after about a week."

Glen spent much of his time viewing parcels of land for sale and imagining how he might develop them. His new wealth made him the subject of several St. Petersburg newspaper articles that described his "rags-to-riches" past; one called him "the taco tycoon." He invested in a shopping center on the island of Tierra Verde, but soon sold it. The property did little to challenge his creativity.

Early in 1970, Glen started a scrapbook of newspaper and magazine articles he considered sources of creative inspiration. Today, these are torn and yellowed, but they reveal the dreams of a newly made millionaire. The clips illustrate ideas or people Glen found intriguing and things he was tempted to buy.

Items include an interview with Walter Knott, founder of Knott's Berry Farm; a photo of a mission-style shopping center under construction in Santa Ana; an article about a corporate-sponsored exhibition of American arts and crafts; a photo of a scale model of a nineteenth-century Italian sailing vessel; and an article that describes how Hamilton, Georgia, had turned its downtown into a museum of turn-of-the-century America. Because of his surname, Glen was drawn to bells, and also in the scrapbook is a letter from a collector who had advertised ninety-eight antique bells for sale in the *Wall Street Journal.*

But before he could begin any collections or build any museums, Glen was called to California. Heavy rains had caused flooding at Taco Bell's Torrance headquarters. "It was such a discouraging time," he recalls. "The water was so deep it covered the desks." As employees sorted through the mess and hung corporate documents to dry on hundreds of racks in a rented warehouse, "We learned which employees would stick by you and which ones got discouraged and wanted to quit."

Despite the setback, the company prospered. Earnings per share and sales per unit were on the rise. The chain continued to expand throughout the southeastern U.S., and a four hundredth Taco Bell would open that summer.

Glen agreed with Robert McKay and John Gorman that Taco Bell should test-market potential menu additions. "Chili, for example," Robert

Bell family archives

Circa 1969. Taco Bell opened a few of these barbecue restaurants in California.

recalls. "But there just weren't enough takers. If you don't sell a lot of it, it's a difficult product to keep fresh on a steam table."

Glen also approved their proposal for "Hickory Bell," a new barbecue-themed fast-food chain. According to Robert, "Taco Bell had an office in Atlanta where the barbecue food is delicious. There was no representation on the West Coast. We were finding properties that were too big for a Taco Bell and thought we could split them in half and use them for two restaurants." The company built a few Hickory Bells in California, but customer response was disappointing. "The losses were pulling us down. So we swallowed our pride, closed up the stores, and concentrated on our golden goose, Taco Bell."

In April 1970, Glen added a *Los Angeles Times* article to his scrapbook: "Make Believe World for Sale: MGM Treasures Going on Auction Block." During thirty-two auctions in May, according to the article, Metro-Gold-wyn-Mayer "will clean its closets and attics of movie props that range from boats and planes to hats and statues . . . including original chariots from *Ben Hur*, an 1878 steam locomotive from *Raintree County*, Andy Hardy's Model A," and other items "from fifty-six years of making more than 2,200 movies." Glen was tempted to attend—and did.

John Galardi recalls, "Glen had energy. He'd keep going until 4 in the morning. At the MGM auctions, he was there ten hours a day."

Glen toured the back lots and alleyways of MGM with multimillionaire bidders, including one of the Hunt brothers. "He had all that money but didn't have a pencil," Glen recalls. "He was continually borrowing mine."

One Polaroid photo Glen took for Marty shows a smiling young woman modeling a pink chiffon ball gown from *Gone With the Wind*. Glen observed bidders compete for a pair of red shoes worn by Judy Garland in *The Wizard of Oz*. The fifteen-thousand-dollar sales price made national news.

He outbid actress Debbie Reynolds for the 1931 Ford Model A roadster Mickey Rooney drove (and repaired) in four Andy Hardy movies. To ease her disappointment, Glen assured her she could borrow it for the museum of movie memorabilia she planned to build. When asked what he intended to do with the items he purchased, Glen replied he thought he might display them at his own museum or perhaps at a theme park.

He successfully bid on a small-scale Viking ship with a fanciful curved prow and an undulating snake on its sail, and a ten-foot model of an eighteenth-century sailing vessel used in *Mutiny on the Bounty*. "The figures of the sailors that came with it were twelve inches tall," Glen recalls. He also bought the uniform Marlon Brando wore in the same film as well as a light blue suit a young Elvis Presley had worn in a mid-sixties movie. "It fit Rex perfectly," Glen recalls.

Glen had reestablished contact with Rex, his son from his first marriage, when his ex-wife Dorothy died in 1965. Ten years earlier, Dorothy had

Hollywood, 1970. At the MGM auction, Glen outbid actress Debbie Reynolds for this 1931 Ford Model A roadster.

married the man she had hired to manage Bell's Hamburgers in San Bernardino.

Rex says, "My stepfather was very jealous, and my dad just stepped out of the picture." In 1964, Dorothy filed for divorce and returned, with fifteen-year-old Rex and his nine-year-old stepbrother, Steve, to Texas to live with her parents. Tragically, for reasons that are still unclear, she committed suicide a few months later.

Bernard Taylor, Rex's grandfather, says, "Glen Bell came right after Dorothy died. He was here for the service, he and his wife. Dorothy's death like to killed us. The best thing for us were the boys. We raised them like our own children." During summers that followed, Rex and Steve visited the Bells in California and later in Florida. Unlike his stepbrother, Gary, who had light brown hair, Rex's was nearly black, and he had inherited the Bell family's large dark eyes. His senior photo shows a handsome youth with a sad smile.

In 1971, the Bells were among the first visitors to Walt Disney World when it opened in Orlando. Glen recalls, "Quite a lot of local people were down on it. They didn't think it would do anything." Glen, however, saw the park's potential and urged Rex to apply for a job. While Rex worked at Disney World, he met and married his first wife, Tricia; their daughter Valerie, Glen's first grandchild, was born in 1974.

Glen arranged for large items from MGM to be stored in California. When he returned to St. Petersburg, his land-hunting expeditions took on new meaning.

"We'd get up in the morning and go exploring," Gary says. "Whenever we walked any piece of property, Dad was constantly evaluating and designing something. It was nonstop. We couldn't walk through some spot without him envisioning a picnic table, people coming there, and the charm of the outdoor experience."

Like Ponce de Leon in search of the Fountain of Youth, Glen sought the perfect piece of Florida real estate. Much of the coast is wetlands, and on one outing, thirteen-year-old Gary sank into mud up to his waist.

"The suction was pretty strong. Dad had to pull me out with a chain around my leg. We had fun on weekends but didn't tell Mom about the quicksand."

Glen narrowed his focus to northern Florida, west of Ocala. According to Gary, "It was cooler there, not swampy like south Florida." As their boat cruised along the tea-dark Withlacoochee River, beneath cypress branches draped with Spanish moss, they spotted a second, smaller river. It fed clear water into the Withlacoochee, and they followed it several miles to its source: a fresh-water spring.

Residents of the nearby town of Dunnellon told them this one, because of the water's shimmering iridescence, was Rainbow Springs. Florida's land mass rests on a reservoir held in place by porous limestone, and Glen and Gary previously had followed streams that disappeared into the ground. When a river did the opposite—it flowed out of the aquifer—it was by definition a natural spring.

A forest dense with cypress, oak, palms, and magnolias surrounded a small lake formed by Rainbow Springs' headwaters; along the shore were a few cabins for rent, a snack bar, and gaily painted glass-bottom boats from which visitors could view underwater wildlife.

Glen recalls a tour guide who repeated in a thick Southern accent, in a melodious sing-song voice, "At beautiful Rainbow Springs you'll find trout and turtles, bass and bream, sunfish and shad, crappie and longnose gar."

Glen adds, "I thought I'd found heaven." He also had found an ideal spot for a family-oriented park.

His sister Dorothy recalls, "Glen had bought a new car, a Ford, and he wanted to show us some property near Dunnellon. He started to go off the road, saying, 'Isn't this nice?' Our mother said, 'You're scratching your new car!' But his imagination was at work; he was thinking real hard."

Marty says the spring "was so clear you could read the fine print on the bottom." But swimming in the water didn't tempt her; it was a chilly seventy-two degrees.

Kathleen, nine, was content to play at the water's edge. One of her favorite memories of Florida is the afternoon her father helped her build a sand castle. "He's always complicating things," she recalls with a smile. "You can't make a simple *quesadilla* with cheese; he'll start chopping tomatoes."

But when Glen sat down next to her in the sand, "It wasn't like he was taking over; he just wanted to improve and expand the castle." Because the wakes of passing boats threatened to flood the structure, Glen modified it with a waterway, moat, and bridges made of twigs. "When he was done, it was really spectacular. It was such an elaborate thing, it looked like a tourist park."

During many visits to Rainbow Springs, Glen and Gary snorkeled in the aquarium-clear water and water-skied along its surface. Viewed from shore, boats appeared suspended in air.

Gary says, "You'd jump off a bridge, and the water was so clear, it was hard to tell when you'd hit the surface." He was determined to explore the spring's source, but when he dove into it, he swam against a current that spilled over 300 million gallons of water per day. "My friends and I held rocks to help us drop."

Despite the volume of water, Glen adds, "The silence kind of surprised me. You expect to hear a bubbling or roaring sound, but it wasn't like a mountain stream." Yet because of abundant wildlife that included frogs, insects, and numerous birds, the spring had its own symphony.

Rainbow Springs, Florida, 1969. Glen and his children: Kathleen, Gary, and Rex.

At night, according to Gary, "We'd stand on a bridge and shine a spot-light into the water. Sometimes we'd see red eyeballs. We figured the farther apart they were, the larger the 'gator."

Glen also recalls snakes: "You had to watch out for them. They'd be in trees overhead, hanging from a limb as well as in the water."

With a population of fifteen hundred, Dunnellon was a small town. Glen soon became friendly with its residents, including the owner of a fish camp (a place to rent cabins and gear) who decided to buy Taco Bell stock. But after the man paid eleven dollars a share, the stock declined to $2.50.

Robert McKay recalls, "The market was deluged with celebrity franchise schemes that were failing." To cash in on the franchise boom, companies had capitalized on famous names—such as Minnie Pearl, Roy Rogers, and Johnny Carson—and started fast-food empires. These soon fizzled because they lacked products with proven consumer appeal, or because they offered inadequate support to franchisees.

Robert adds, "The stock market has a herd philosophy. It was guilt by association. We were in a less-favored industry. Yet Taco Bell was making money. We were making progress."

A few savvy investors researched the company and consumer dining trends, and decided Taco Bell's stock was a bargain.

According to Lester Morris of Mesirow Financial, a Chicago investment firm, "My specialty was finding small companies with potential. I had no bias. There were skeptics; some thought the popularity of Mexican food in America was a fad. We looked at Taco Bell sales volumes and were impressed. Stores in out-of-the-way places did well without mass-market advertising. McCormick Spice introduced a line of Mexican spices, which confirmed an inherent growing demand for Mexican food."

Robert recalls, "Les and his clients bought Taco Bell stock. Before long, we were back up to five dollars a share. Anybody who bought in at two or three dollars made an unbelievable amount of money." Lester Morris later joined Taco Bell's board of directors.

Fortunately, the fish camp owner held onto his stock. Glen recalls, "A couple of years later, he told me, laughing, 'You've paid for my new home.'"

Rainbow Springs itself was not for sale. Holiday Inn and S&H Green Stamps owned it and planned to develop it as a tourist attraction. Another project that would bring visitors to the area was the proposed Cross Florida Barge Canal, so Glen purchased thirty acres that bordered the Rainbow River. The December 17, 1970 edition of the *Dunnellon Press* described his plans to build a five-hundred-seat deluxe restaurant in addition to a Mexican gift shop and snack bar.

Four months later, the same newspaper ran a photo of a smiling Glen standing on the deck of "a prototype electric-powered 'flower boat' patterned after the famous boats of Mexico City, which feature holiday dining and sightseeing." Glen had been captivated by the idea since he first observed the boats, years earlier, on Lake Xochimilco ("*Zo-chee-MIL-koh*"). Glen's custom-made vessel resembled a small houseboat with large screened windows. Garlands of carved, painted flowers decorated the roofline, and colorful geometric patterns enhanced the sides.

"We came down the river one evening with lights on the Xochimilco boat," Glen recalls. "The reflections on the water were beautiful."

But before Glen completed his plans for the Dunnellon property, President Nixon halted work on the barge canal for ecological reasons. About the same time, Glen found a spring farther north that was just as appealing as Rainbow Springs—and that was for sale.

Fanning Springs is west of Gainesville near the town of Chiefland. Glen bought 160 acres that included the spring and surrounding land as well as an old motel. The wife of the couple who sold it to Glen showed Marty stacks of bed linens and explained, in detail, how to tend the guest rooms. Marty says, "I didn't have the heart to tell her that Glen planned to tear it down."

Of Florida's three-hundred-plus springs, the best known is on the outskirts of Ocala; Silver Springs releases 550 million gallons of water per day. At eighty million gallons, Fanning Springs is considerably smaller, "yet it produces enough water to serve a city the size of Los Angeles," Glen says. His acreage bordered both Highway 19 and the Suwannee River, which intersects Fanning Springs one hundred yards from its head.

The Suwannee originates two hundred miles north in the Okefenokee Swamp of southern Georgia and is famous because of a song Stephen Foster wrote in 1850: *Old Folks at Home.* ("Way down upon the Suwannee River . . . ") At the point the Suwannee meets Fanning Springs, according to Gary, the river forms a warm black blanket above the colder spring water. He would hold his breath and dive beneath the Suwannee, then follow the clear water for several yards until it darkened and disappeared.

Glen says, "The Suwannee is a nice big river. You could go fifty miles and never see another boat. It was ideal for water skiing. I was going to have paddle boats on the river. They'd go around a bend to different little villages along the bank. Mexican, Italian, each would have a different atmosphere, with its own motel, restaurant, some kind of entertainment, and shops. You'd get off the tour boat, visit one village, then go on to another. Guests could come by car from the highway or by boat from the river."

But Glen's plans became tangled with bureaucratic red tape, and it soon became evident his dream might take years to materialize—if ever.

He also learned "you can't keep a beautiful spot to yourself." Trespassers toting picnic baskets arrived at Fanning Springs and told him, "We have our family reunion here every year." Church groups assembled for baptisms, and the idyllic setting attracted itinerant "flower children."

One weekend, campers who thought they had found a secluded oasis suddenly were in the midst of a party Glen had approved, hosted by the governor of Florida. "He came down the river with twenty or thirty boats. About a thousand people showed up."

In the summer of 1972, the Bells decided to drive across the United States. Miss Bradley, who stayed in Florida, approved of the trip; she enjoyed nothing so much as travel and had wondered why the Bells didn't travel more. It came as a surprise to her, however, when Glen called a few weeks later, informed her he had bought property in Oregon, and told her his family would move there.

She recalls, "He asked if I would move with them, and I replied, 'Of course.' "

Miss Bradley made arrangements to ship the Bells' household possessions and sell their Florida properties. Today, both Fanning Springs and Rainbow Springs are state parks.

During the next two years, the Bells owned homes in Roseburg, Oregon, south of Eugene; and in Witter Springs, near Lower Clearlake, in Northern California. Glen purchased the properties as he indulged a favorite pastime: driving through the countryside and viewing land for sale. Glen's aunt Edna lived in Portland, and he bought his mother a home near her sister.

According to Glen's sister Dorothy, "I think they were looking for the best place in the world to live." In Roseburg, "Glen owned quite a bit of land, with horses and chickens. It was so much fun. Marty hatched baby chicks in the kitchen. The kids loved it, but it rained a lot."

Glen was amused when their furniture arrived from Florida. "While the moving van was unloaded, out rolled Miss Bradley's black Cadillac."

Gary remembers Roseburg as "a logging town in a rural area. We were there five months. We lived in a double-wide mobile home on property Dad had bought—150 acres that included a great long ridge with a view of Roseburg.

"What brought us to Witter Springs must have been the setting. It was the most spectacular place I've known for natural beauty. Dad owned about fifty acres, and we had horses. The living room faced a bend in the river, and there was a little bridge across it and a pond. You could walk out into the apple orchard with a tree trimmer and make clipping sounds, and deer would come. They loved apple branches, and they'd stand there and eat them."

Glen says, "We left Clearlake because Marty didn't care for the winter. It was the worst they'd ever had. It got down to seven degrees, and the pipes froze."

His life-long friend, Neal Baker, claims he's "partly responsible" for the Bells' return to Southern California. "They were living in Clearlake, and Glen asked me, 'Where's that place you said, if you ever had enough money, you'd want to live? I'd like to look at it.' So Glen flew into an airport near San Bernardino, and I drove him down to Rancho Santa Fe."

Located in north San Diego county, Rancho Santa Fe is known worldwide as a haven for the quietly rich. Tucked amid a eucalyptus forest are sprawling ranch-style homes on multiacre lots. Narrow roads wind along cliff tops, homes have views of canyons and the distant sea, and gates across tree-lined driveways swing open only to invited guests. Yet there's no flash and dazzle.

"Everyone there has it made," says Miss Bradley. "But they don't show off their money."

Glen bought a home on Via Fortuna and joined the local Rotary Club. His secretary established an office in Rancho Santa Fe's small business district where the architecture is Spanish and red bougainvillea flows along stucco walls into sunny courtyards.

"What really brought them there was the weather," says Gary, who was seventeen at the time. Rancho Santa Fe's rainfall is minimal, and temperatures seldom exceed ninety degrees in summer or drop below forty in winter.

Gary adds, "I got a job as a bag boy at Ashley's Market; it paid two dollars an hour. I learned you don't slam the trunk on a Lincoln or a Rolls Royce. You lower it, and it slowly closes by itself."

But at fifty, Glen was not ready to retire. In the fall of 1974, he found out a former lumber mill with a narrow-gauge railway was for sale in Northern California. By 1975, Glen was the proud owner of two turn-of-the-century steam locomotives and 340 acres of land, much of which resembled his childhood home of Cedar Springs.

He intended to use the property to develop a railroad-oriented theme park, complete with a lake and Xochimilco boats, where families could travel together back in time.

Glen's Recipes for Success

#43: Smart investors know the difference between a fad and an idea whose time has come.

A lot of people assumed Mexican fast food was a fad that would have its day then disappear. When our stock dropped because of a widespread lack of confidence in franchised restaurants, investors were cautious. The few who researched consumer trends, studied our financial statements, and recognized the company's strengths bought Taco Bell stock at bargain prices—and eventually made a fortune.

#44: Wealth shouldn't change your values, but it does give you freedom to pursue your dreams.

It's the nature of innovators to want to move on to other things. When Taco Bell was established and in the hands of good managers, I was free to pursue a number of exciting options. The challenge was to spend my resources, time, and talents in ways that maximized all three.

#45: Be on the lookout for people and ideas that inspire you.

How you spend your time and money illustrates what's important to you and what sort of person you are. Ideally, wealth and opportunity will bring out the best in you. One way to keep your goals in front of you is to save articles that describe causes, activities, and people whom you admire. But remember, a person isn't truly successful until he handles success wisely.

CHAPTER FOURTEEN

Westside & Cherry Valley Railway
1974-1977

WHEN GLEN BOUGHT THE WESTSIDE & CHERRY VALLEY RAILWAY, its 340 acres included a thirty-acre mill pond, two antique trains, and nine miles of weed-infested tracks.

At the time, the population of the town of Tuolumne ("*Tuh-WAH-luh-mē*"), located on the western slopes of the Sierras 120 miles east of San Francisco, was fifteen hundred—less than during the Gold Rush era a century earlier.

Before it closed in 1960, the West Side Flume and Lumber Company had been Tuolumne's largest employer. In its heyday, the mill's narrow-gauge railway rattled between Tuolumne and Cherry Valley on Yosemite's western border—a crow-fly distance of eighteen miles.

As Glen walked terrain fragrant with pine and cedar, he envisioned an idyllic village with shops, restaurants, and a farmer's market—the sort of American town that might have existed had there been no Great Depression. His historic park would preserve all that was worth remembering from the 1930s: an unhurried pace of life; people who were polite and friendly; and a serene and gentle time before television, illegal drugs, and antiwar demonstrations. To make the back-in-time experience vivid, buildings and furnishings would be true to the period. Only early-century cars and trucks or horse-drawn wagons would roll along the roadways.

On the mill pond would float an assortment of vintage vessels, including paddle wheel steamers, Chinese sampans, and Xochimilco flower boats. These would serve various destinations around the shoreline, each with a different theme: country town, logging camp, and Mexican, Indian, and Chinese settlements.

Tuolumne newspapers referred to Glen as a "developer," which was unfortunate because by the mid-1970s the word had taken on a negative connotation. Residents were aware that not all land developers could be trusted to respect an area's heritage and natural beauty, and they worried that the railway would be turned into a carnival or strewn with homes that appeared stamped from an assembly line.

One resident told the town newspaper, "We live here because we like the isolation. This whole project just seems like another tourist trap."

Others viewed a developer as someone who deserved to be fleeced, should the opportunity arise.

But most residents of Tuolumne were relieved when word got out the founder of Taco Bell had bought the mill property. Because the town had yet to recover from the mill closing fifteen years earlier, "Half of Tuolumne was on welfare," Glen recalls.

One Tuolumne native wrote the newspaper: "I stacked lumber in that yard for years. When they closed the mill, people said there'd be grass growing in the streets of Tuolumne. I'm glad to see this happening. It gives my kids a chance at a future here."

Glen looked forward to an opportunity to improve the town's economy and create jobs. "In general, I don't like to just give money to people. I feel that robs them of their pride. It's better if they earn it."

The Bells bought a house in nearby Sonora, a Gold Rush city with a Victorian-era downtown. They kept their home in Rancho Santa Fe, where Kathleen, fifteen, attended high school. Kathleen was reluctant to move, and her parents did not insist.

Glen and Marty decided to live alternately in each location: two weeks in Northern California and two weeks in Southern California. "We were in airplanes a lot," Glen recalls. Although the Pacific Southwest Airlines (PSA) flight from San Diego to San Francisco lasted less than an hour, Marty adds, "getting to Sonora was an all-day trip." A shuttle from San Francisco first flew farther east to Yosemite before it landed at a small airport near

Sonora. Other options were to drive from San Diego (eight hours), or rent a car in San Francisco—but there was no place in Sonora to return the vehicle.

While Kathleen's parents were away, her widowed grandfather, Harl Ahl, came from Redlands and stayed with her. Miss Bradley continued to maintain Glen's business affairs at the Rancho Santa Fe office. Gary, eighteen, went to live with Grandma Bell, who had moved from Oregon to Cedar City, Utah, to be near a favorite niece.

"It was great," Gary recalls. "I'd wake up to the smell of bacon. Grandma loved to have someone to cook for, and I loved to eat, so we were a magic team. It was a perfect arrangement. When I worked construction, she'd fix me lunch."

In July 1975, Glen resigned as chairman of the board of Taco Bell (he remained on its Board of Directors) and in Taco Bell's secondary public offering sold 450,000 shares of stock at thirteen dollars a share—for a total of $5.85 million.

In a *Wall Street Journal* interview, Taco Bell president Robert McKay assured company stockholders, "As far as changes in day-to-day management, there are none."

The *Journal* also reported that the offering was "oversubscribed"—which was good news for Taco Bell. Robert recalls, "It meant people put in more orders to buy, based on the preliminary prospectus, than there was stock available. It sure helped the aftermarket price. Buyers who couldn't get in bought stock one to five days after the offering, which pushed the price up."

Glen retained 24.2 percent ownership of Taco Bell and continued to be its largest shareholder.

Around the same time, he gave a speech to the Rancho Santa Fe Rotary Club. "I am truly grateful to live in a country where people can start at the bottom and succeed," Glen told the assembly. "Taco Bell now has 625 stores in 35 states. We opened sixty-three new Taco Bells last year. Sales exceeded $84 million, an increase of 19 percent over the previous year."

Although he was proud of Taco Bell and also was its primary owner, Glen did not attend board meetings or visit the corporate offices. According to Robert, "After we moved from the ugly building in Torrance—we built on Redhill, in Irvine—Glen and I talked on the phone. I told him the offices looked great. They were all set up. But when he came to town, he told me to meet him in a back booth of Denny's. I said, 'Come and see the offices,' and he said OK, but it was hard to pin him down.

"One day Glen said, 'I'll bring Marty. Let's have dinner.' So we met for dinner in Irvine. Around 10 P.M. I said, 'Ready to see the offices?' Glen said, 'What time do the people leave?' I told him ten or eleven at the latest. He said, 'Let's have more coffee. Let's wait a while.' I thought, uh-oh, knowing Glen, we'll be here til midnight. When we finally got to the office, I turned on all the lights and let him go. When he was done looking around, he told me, 'This is really gorgeous,' and there were tears in his eyes."

Despite Taco Bell's growth, by the mid-seventies, only one menu item had been added to Glen's original five: an enchilada-burrito hybrid Robert McKay and John Gorman named the *enchirito*. A photo of a circa-1975 menu board shows it priced at seventy-four cents, with this description: "EN-CHI-REE-TOH: Quality ground beef cooked in Taco Bell's own famous sauce, tasty pinto beans, chopped onions, folded in a soft flour tortilla covered with mild red sauce, shredded cheddar cheese, and topped with olive slices." The item was discontinued during the 1980s, but a "bring back the enchirito" movement among Taco Bell fans continues to this day.

America celebrated its bicentennial the year Glen took possession of the mill property, and patriotism, which had become unfashionable during the Vietnam War, again was in vogue.

In March 1976, shortly after Glen told Tuolumne's local newspaper his purpose in buying the land was to "build a historic park" that would "recreate Tuolumne's early logging days," county planning commissioners voted unanimously to approve zoning changes that, according to a later article, "will pave the way for the development of a multimillion-dollar tourist attraction." Glen promised that no carnival rides would be included, and he invited locals to share photos, films, and memories of the logging operation. On May 12, he drove an antique Mack truck in the town's Mother Lode Roundup parade.

A Tuolumne resident who shared Glen's enthusiasm for antique vehicles was Joe Speaker, owner of one of the town's three gas stations. Joe was near retirement age, and Glen offered to buy his service station with the intent to convert it to a garage for the restoration of old cars and trucks. When

Tuolumne, California, 1976. Babushka, a stray dog found on the railway, adopted Glen.

Glen asked Joe to supervise the renovated garage's operations, the older man told the town newspaper, "I feel like I've died and gone to heaven."

But not all of Tuolumne residents were so supportive. That summer, according to the local newspaper, the town's volunteer fire department extinguished "a small grass fire . . . deliberately set" on the Westside property. After a second fire was followed by vandalism of fences and earth-moving equipment, Glen hired a security guard.

That fall, a grinning Joe accompanied Glen to an auction of vehicles offered by casino owner Bill Harrah in Nevada. Glen recalls, "Harrah had the biggest collection anywhere. It was almost overwhelming. There were rows and rows of spic-and-span cars. The shop was a showplace, too, and the mechanics wore white coats." Glen bought two tour buses once used at Yellowstone National Park. "I was mostly interested in work vehicles."

As word spread that Glen wanted antique trucks, buses, and delivery wagons, his collection grew to over twenty-five vehicles, including a 1910 American La-France fire engine; a 1923 Dodge screen-side pickup truck; and a 1909 Renault limousine—in addition to the Model A Ford he had bought earlier from MGM. Glen also purchased a 1919 White truck

Glenn Tyra

Tuolumne, 1976. This photo of Glen operating a bulldozer ran in the Tuolumne Prospector. *Domed tower is a former sawdust burner.*

similar to the one that had brought his parents and siblings to Cedar Springs in 1935.

In mid-October 1976, two county supervisors at a public meeting criticized the proposed Westside project, intimating "the developer's" intent was not to benefit the community but rather to exploit it. They pointed out that Glen had turned down a request to pay the cost of improving roads, installing stop signs, and making other improvements to the local infrastructure—expenses the town would have to shoulder if the historic park became a reality.

Glen suspected their motivation was to gain publicity a few weeks prior to an election, and admitted, in a written statement to the press, that he was perplexed and angry. He listed benefits the town might reasonably anticipate from the Westside project, including historic preservation, jobs, and an improved economy.

"I was looking forward to sharing this experience with Tuolumne County," he wrote, then added, if "forced to abandon the project," he

Bell family archives

1977. Mill pond, West Side & Cherry Valley Railway. Boat in foreground is powered by a "steam donkey."

promised to leave the property "in a condition that will be an asset to the community."

Several days later, the supervisors met and agreed that Glen would not be responsible to build roads or otherwise improve county land outside the boundaries of his property.

On November 3, the Tuolumne newspaper ran a front-page photo of a bulldozer grading land at Westside & Cherry Valley. In the background is a remnant of the old mill, a dome-topped tower once used to burn sawdust. Though his face is in shadow, it's obvious by the wide shoulders and cowboy hat that Glen is the equipment operator.

Marty recalls, "As they arranged rocks and water in the mill pond, I panned for gold." All of Tuolumne County is riddled with abandoned gold mines, and waterways still yield occasional nuggets.

She adds, "When work was slow at the mill, the employees used to get thirty-six inches of space each along the Tuolumne River to pan for gold.

It gave them enough to buy groceries during a lean time." Then, as now, local residents show their children how to scoop dirt from a streambed with a shallow pan, slosh it beneath the water's surface, then pick out tiny gleams of gold.

Marty says she "didn't get much, just a handful of crumbs, but it was exciting."

In the meantime, Glen sought different treasure. The December 6, 1976, edition of the *Washington Post* describes an auction of architectural antiques in Los Angeles he attended with Westside's general manager, Jim Summers. "We bid up to $26,000 for an early-century drug store," Jim told the newspaper. "But it went for $27,500." Glen successfully bid $4,750 for two 10-foot-diameter clocks originally from the Bradford Exchange Railway Station in England.

By Christmas, the 1913 Shay locomotive once used by the lumber company was back in operation. A Westside employee costumed as Santa Claus rode into Tuolumne aboard it, to the delight of local children. Five months later, the *Modesto Bee* newspaper reported that Westside & Cherry Valley Railway's east loop track had opened: "Once again sixty-four-year-old narrow-gauge engine No. 15 blasted its deep-throated steam whistle as it clickety-clacked over a half-mile of railroad track through the hills of picturesque Tuolumne."

Glen recalls, "People in town told me that when they heard the old whistle blow, they got tears in their eyes." Also recently completed was a 7,200-square-foot engine house for the sixty-ton locomotive; and in the works, the restoration of an 1899 Sterns steam locomotive.

News from Utah, however, turned Glen's attention to more urgent matters: His mother's health was failing. Gary had been with Grandma Bell, and had called an ambulance, when she experienced a mild heart attack. Ruth was seventy-five.

Although Glen had been generous with his mother, providing her with money, housing, and trips abroad, she had never asked her oldest son for anything—even after she had learned, to her surprise and disbelief, that he was a millionaire.

But this time, when he asked what he could do for her, Ruth replied, "I'd like to have the family together again." Her children had not been with her, all in one place at the same time, since she lived in Cedar Springs.

1976. Glen at the throttle of his restored 1913 Shay locomotive.

Glen riding the cowcatcher of the Shay.

1977. Glen's restored 1899 Sterns steam locomotive crosses a trestle.

With Glen's financial assistance and the help of Miss Bradley, Glen's older sister Deloris arranged for family members to meet in August 1977 at a resort in San Diego. Then known as Vacation Village, the bayside hotel consists of Spanish-style cottages tucked within a tropical landscape that resembles a Florida botanical park. Photos taken at the three-day event show Ruth with her six grown children and sixteen grandchildren. In one photo, Ruth is seated with her purse on her lap. Her dark eyes sparkle, but she looks tired. Atop her head is a tiara.

"We crowned her 'The Queen' at the reunion," Deloris says.

Courtesy of Deloris Lukens

San Diego, 1977. Ruth Bell.

Afterward, at her home in Banning, California, Deloris tended her mother as Ruth's health worsened. In November 1977, all six siblings again assembled in one place—for their mother's funeral. Their grief, according to Deloris, was easier to bear because their mother had been granted her final wish.

Glen returned to Westside & Cherry Valley as construction neared completion on a 1930s-era train depot. According to the newspaper, a playground in downtown Tuolumne, built with funds donated by "the Westside railway project," also had opened. Westside's work force numbered fifty, with estimations of an eventual five hundred.

Sonora resident Frank Cimino quit his job as a schoolteacher to work at Westside. He recalls, "I can still see Mr. Bell sitting on the depot deck, eating a chili dog, looking at the scenery and watching what was going on. I remember him with his wife, talking with the staff and enjoying the view. He was someone everyone at Westside thoroughly enjoyed."

Gordon Ham, another former Westside employee, agrees. "Glen Bell was great to work for—and considerate. But he could be lackadaisical about money. One day our financial manager asked, 'Anybody see Mr. Bell?' He was out on the grounds. For three or four days, he'd been carrying a check in his pocket that was needed to meet payroll and bills. It hadn't dawned on him. The financial manager said, 'Get that man in here!' "

Gordon adds, "Glen Bell was very generous with the Tuolumne Historical Society, and he spent considerable money on the county fair. He liked the area, and the people liked him."

Yet in December 1977, when the 1899 Sterns steam locomotive chugged into service at Westside—and more than seven hundred Tuolumne residents were treated to a ride—letters to the editor of the local paper protested the amount of fuel that would be "wasted" by the park's trains.

"I felt discouraged," Glen says. "Instead of good guys restoring things, we were bad guys using fuel."

Glen also realized that to complete Westside & Cherry Valley the way he had envisioned it would take more resources than originally estimated. In the two years he had owned the property, he had spent several million dollars, and the park was not yet ready to open to the public. It would take at least a decade, and many more millions of dollars, before it was finished. On the one hand, he wanted to hurry its completion; on the other, he wondered if it was worth the risk.

"To do it right, $20 million would have ensured its success," Glen recalls. "If it made you the good guy to spend it, the temptation was to go ahead." But if he continued, he would have to liquidate part or all of his ownership of Taco Bell.

As Glen weighed his options, he received a phone call from a representative of Bateman Eichler, Hill Richards, a Los Angeles brokerage firm that had handled both Taco Bell stock offerings. The broker advised Glen that H. J. Heinz, a food manufacturing company headquartered in Pittsburgh, was interested in adding a fast-food restaurant chain to its holdings. Would Glen consider selling Taco Bell to H. J. Heinz, if the company made an acceptable offer?

Glen hesitated, then replied, "Yes."

Glen's Recipes for Success

#46: We're fortunate we live in a country in which anyone, with hard work, persistence, and determination, can become a millionaire.

It's easy to take the benefits of living in America for granted and to forget it's much harder elsewhere for children of poor families to become wealthy. Capitalism and the free enterprise system will work for anyone determined to pursue them.

#47: If you give people money when they've done nothing to earn it, you create dependence and rob them of their pride.

Instead of being resourceful and industrious, some people prefer to take it easy and be taken care of. You may be tempted to give them money because they've asked for it and need it. But doing so rewards their lack of initiative. Instead, help them find ways to earn an income.

#48: Use your ideas and resources to benefit others.

One reward of hard work is wealth, and those who earn it are entitled to enjoy it. But don't assume you'll be happy because you're able to purchase anything you please. It may be fun for a while, but eventually it leads to an empty feeling. Wealth brings happiness when it's combined with ingenuity to enrich the lives of others.

CHAPTER FIFTEEN

Battle for the Bell
January 1978

EARLY IN JANUARY 1978, Robert McKay, president of Taco Bell, was on a business trip when he received an urgent phone call.

Robert recalls that his secretary told him, "There's something crazy going on with the stock. It's all the way up to thirty dollars." During the previous week, Taco Bell's stock had hovered around twenty-six dollars a share.

"Analysts had called and asked what was going on," Robert says. "There were rumors a sale was in the works. I told the *Los Angeles Times* there was no truth to it. Taco Bell was not for sale."

But when Robert returned to Taco Bell's corporate headquarters in Irvine and spoke with Glen on the phone, "I found out everything."

Glen says, "It was hard to break the news to McKay. I knew he wasn't interested in selling. He was doing a great job running the company, and he enjoyed it."

On Saturday January 7, Robert flew to Oakland, a city across the bay from San Francisco. "I didn't know where Tuolumne was. Glen and I met at an airport coffee shop. I was still in an emotional state. I asked him, 'Glen, why did you do it? Why didn't you talk to me first?' He said, 'Bob, I was afraid you'd talk me out of it.'"

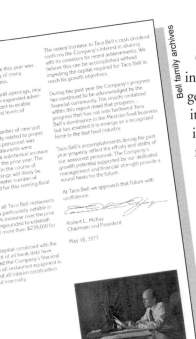

The recent increase in Taco Bell's cash dividend confirms the Company's interest in sharing with its investors its recent achievements. We believe this can be accomplished without impeding the capital required for Taco Bell to reach its growth objectives.

During the past year the Company's progress has continued to be acknowledged by the financial community. The results contained within this report detail that progress... progress that has not only furthered Taco Bell's dominance in the Mexican food business but has enabled it to emerge as a recognized force in the fast food industry.

Taco Bell's accomplishments during the past year properly reflect the efforts and ability of our seasoned personnel. The Company's growth potential supported by our dedicated management and financial strength provide a sound basis for the future.

At Taco Bell we approach that future with confidence.

Robert L. McKay
Chairman and President

May 18, 1977

1977. Taco Bell's impressive annual report made the company a desirable acquisition.

Glen explains when he learned H. J. Heinz was interested in Taco Bell, "I felt relieved. Taco Bell was getting bigger and bigger. I felt it was time to turn it over to a national company that could direct its growth and knew how to help it realize its full potential."

"I might not have talked Glen out of it," Robert says. "But if he had asked my opinion, I would have told him I felt the sale was premature. We had the momentum of a developing company. Taco Bell would have more value in a few years. I was happy at the time. Why get out early? Why not maximize yours and the shareholders' potential? Why sell unless you're at a precipice and things are about to fall apart? We were opening eighty stores a year, and had fewer problems than ever."

Of course, from a buyer's perspective, Taco Bell's growth and stability were precisely what made the company attractive.

Taco Bell's 1977 annual report, a twenty-eight-page booklet illustrated with photos of tomatoes studded with water droplets, smiling employees in gold polyester uniforms, and families seated at orange Formica tables, also included a photo of Robert McKay at work behind a gleaming hardwood desk.

In his letter to shareholders, Robert wrote: "Average unit sales for all Taco Bell restaurants increased 27 percent. This is particularly notable in view of last year's 30 percent increase over the prior year. These gains compounded to establish average unit sales of more than $239,000 for the year." For the nine months ending November 30, 1977, corporate revenues increased to $82.7 million from $63.5 million in the same period during the prior year. Earnings per share were $2.31 compared to $1.93. Return on shareholders' equity was an impressive 36 percent.

The annual report also stated that eighty-six Taco Bells opened for a total of 759 in thirty-eight states. Of these, 329 were company-operated, and 430 were franchised. Employees numbered 7,000. Menu additions included the

1977. Taco Bell's menu board at the time of the PepsiCo merger.

Burrito Supreme and the Beefy Tostada—and all food items still sold for less than one dollar.

After he spoke with a representative of Taco Bell's brokerage firm in December 1977, Glen flew to Los Angeles. He signed a proxy agreement that allowed Bateman Eichler, Hill Richards to broker his ownership of Taco Bell.

In the meantime, H. J. Heinz contracted with Bill Tilley, a Taco Bell investor, franchisee, and CPA with offices on Wilshire Boulevard. As H. J. Heinz's "investment advisor," Bill would expedite the sale, and Heinz would pay him a half-million-dollar commission.

"I also shared in the Bateman transaction," Bill recalls. "It was an exchange for putting them on the Heinz contract."

Bill says the sale of Taco Bell to Heinz seemed like a win-win situation, partly because Taco Bell used quantities of tomato sauce, one of H. J. Heinz's specialties. Moreover, "Heinz brought in a group of MBAs to evaluate the entire fast food industry, and they said the best growth was in Mexican food."

Yet before negotiations began, Glen's accountant cautioned him that if he sold his holdings in Taco Bell, he would end up paying half of whatever amount he received in taxes. Glen owned 24.2 percent of the company, which at the current market price per share was close to $20 million. After taxes, it would be $10 million.

But Glen had signed a contract that gave Bateman Eichler the go-ahead to begin negotiations. He realized if he was going to protect his assets, he needed the best possible legal counsel. He retained Grover Hyler, an expert in corporate affairs and senior partner of Latham & Watkins, one of the world's largest law firms.

Glen recalls, "Hyler and I went to Bateman Eichler's plush offices together. Everyone knew who he was and knew his reputation. Bateman Eichler wanted to jump the gun on the sale to Heinz, but when they saw me with Hyler, they realized I had a strong person on my side."

Hyler had reviewed Glen's agreement with Bateman Eichler and saw that it was binding only if the sale to Heinz took place. Also, Glen had final approval of the terms of the sale. There was nothing in Glen's agreement with Bateman Eichler that required a cash transaction—which left open an important alternative that Hyler realized could protect Glen from a whopping tax liability.

The attorney told Bateman Eichler's representatives he had advised Glen, in order to avoid capital gains taxes, that the only acceptable transaction was an exchange of stock: Glen should trade his ownership in Taco Bell for an equally valued amount of stock in the purchasing corporation—which did not necessarily have to be Heinz.

"Glen was brilliantly advised by Hyler," Bill Tilley admits.

Hyler had raised the intriguing possibility that another company might compete with H. J. Heinz and make a better offer. If Taco Bell had to be sold, Robert McKay reasoned, it might as well go to the highest bidder. "When Glen indicated he wanted to sell the business, my job was not to fight him but to make sure we sold to a good company."

Glen agreed it would be ideal for Taco Bell to be purchased by a corporation that would nurture further expansion and that understood the fast-food industry. It also would be in the best interests of Taco Bell shareholders to trade their stock for that of a stable, growing company.

Robert recalls, "I asked Glen, 'Would you let me see what I can do to get a better deal? It'll take a week or ten days.'" The companies Robert contacted that indicated an interest in Taco Bell included R. J. Reynolds, Quaker Oats, Heinz, and Beatrice Foods. He left Los Angeles on Saturday, January 14.

"R. J. Reynolds was so big in the tobacco business it didn't seem like the right fit. At Palmer House in Chicago, I met with the head of Beatrice Foods. They were awfully big, and I wasn't convinced they would make Taco Bell a priority.

"Then I went to Chicago's merchandise mart and met with the chairman of Quaker Oats. He joked, 'I didn't realize Taco Bell was so big. Maybe you should acquire us instead of us acquiring you.'

"Heinz sent a corporate jet to pick me up, like in the movies, and flew me to Pittsburgh, where I talked with their president and the chairman of the board. I didn't favor Heinz. They were an old, well-respected company, but I didn't feel their stock had the potential growth I was looking for."

H. J. Heinz, however, ignored Robert's polite refusal. The company's president and advisors flew to Los Angeles. Because Glen did not share

Robert's misgivings about H. J. Heinz, and was hopeful an exchange of stock might be arranged, he asked John Gorman, Taco Bell's former vice president and director of operations, to represent him at the meetings.

John says, "I had left Taco Bell a few weeks earlier to go with a new company, in an unrelated field, that was just starting to franchise."

But by this time, Bill Tilley recalls, "The *Wall Street Journal* had been running front-page stories about Taco Bell. There were rumors everywhere."

Robert received a phone call from Don Kendall, chairman of PepsiCo. "He wanted to know what was going on, because PepsiCo might be interested in acquiring Taco Bell." The merger was especially attractive to PepsiCo because Taco Bell was the company's largest cola syrup and Mountain Dew customer. Robert was optimistic; PepsiCo had shown strong growth in soft drinks and snack foods and recently had expanded into the fast-food marketplace.

While PepsiCo's top management discussed the merits of a merger with Taco Bell, executives of several other equally interested corporations boarded flights to Los Angeles. Men in tailored pinstripe suits carrying expensive leather briefcases converged on the same Orange County hotel chosen by H. J. Heinz. Glen and his representatives also were there, and it soon became the epicenter of a bidding war.

Glen recalls, "The companies occupied suites of rooms on several floors. Every time you got into the elevator, you'd see attorneys from Heinz, or maybe one of the principals of Beatrice Foods or Campbell Soup. The suspense and tension were incredible."

Bill adds, "Tension? Oh, God, yes. People in that business, that's what they live for. I was trying to concentrate on seeing the transaction completed in the most favorable terms. At the hotel, we wanted to avoid competitors, not run into them. Glen kept insisting the transaction be tax-deferred, but the Heinz acquisition team said the board would not ratify a stock exchange deal."

According to John Gorman, "It was cloak and dagger. Bateman Eichler's representative and I would go to meetings in the middle of the night. We were frisked by security guards to make sure we didn't have tape recorders hidden on us. Then I'd call Glen and tell him what was happening."

In the meantime, Glen waited in a hotel room, drank coffee, and tried to stay calm.

John says negotiations "reached an impasse on Wednesday or Thursday. The president of Heinz threatened, 'If we don't reach a favorable conclusion, we're going to do a hostile takeover.'" In other words, Heinz would proceed without the approval of Taco Bell's board of directors.

Bill concurs. "If Heinz went hostile, they were going to file with the Securities and Exchange Commission on Monday morning at 7, Washington, D.C. time, to tender an offer to acquire controlling interest in the company."

"Heinz was very serious," Glen adds. "If the deal didn't go their way, they were going to be spoilers."

Andrall ("Andy") Pearson, president of PepsiCo at the time, recalls that when he heard H. J. Heinz might attempt an unfriendly takeover, "we dropped everything" and flew from New York to Los Angeles.

Glen discussed PepsiCo's potential with Robert McKay. "Pepsi had grown a lot in the preceding five years," Glen recalls. The company's soft drinks were distributed to 140 countries worldwide, and PepsiCo owned Frito-Lay (which included snack foods such as Fritos, Doritos, Cheetos, Lay's, and Ruffles). PepsiCo's new restaurant division had acquired Pizza Hut a few months earlier, in November 1977.

With Glen's approval, Robert met with PepsiCo representatives at Taco Bell corporate offices on Saturday, January 28.

Robert says, "Andy brought Frank Carney, founder of Pizza Hut, and Bob Dettmer, Pepsi's chief financial officer. Don Kendall was on vacation but followed our negotiations closely by phone."

Andy recalls that Robert "was interested in having Taco Bell 'in the right hands' and getting the highest bid." And, of course, negotiating a stock transfer instead of a cash sale.

When PepsiCo offered thirty-two dollars a share, Robert phoned Glen. According to Andy, "Bob said he checked with Bell, and they wanted more. After a brief discussion with Kendall, I made a final offer."

It was a generous one, designed to bring negotiations to a close. Robert says, "Because of Heinz, Dettmer and Pearson wanted to get everything wrapped up by Monday morning. We started talking Saturday at noon and shook hands at 4 P.M. on Sunday."

The sales price was an astonishing thirty-seven dollars a share. But by the time the merger was consummated the following May, Taco Bell's stock had jumped to forty-seven dollars. "Pepsi's stock was selling at thirty-three dollars," Robert says. "We received 1.43 shares of Pepsi for every share of Taco Bell."

Robert chose Merrill Lynch to broker the transaction, and when the papers were signed, Glen became PepsiCo's largest individual shareholder with approximately 1 percent of the company's stock. Moreover, because a corporation's shareholders are its owners, when Glen sold Taco Bell, he continued to "own" the company he founded.

Robert adds, "The sales price the *L. A. Times* reported, $125 million, was an estimate; $130 million is more accurate." Glen's share of that amount was slightly less than one-fourth, or about $32 million.

Yet acquaintances who assumed Glen had owned 100 percent of Taco Bell thought his wealth was far greater.

When he heard about the sale, entertainer Phil Crosby was having lunch with another of Glen's former El Taco partners, Harland Svare. "Harland and I and Frank Fuller, another Rams player (now deceased), were at the Luau Restaurant on Rodeo Drive. Harland was laughing, and I said, 'Tell me what's so funny. Let me in on the joke.'

"He said, 'Glen Bell just sold Taco Bell to PepsiCo, the whole kit and kaboodle.' I said, 'That's great, how much did he get for it?' When Harland told me, '$125 million,' I choked on my drink. I had to put the glass down.

"If we'd stayed with Glen, if Harland and I had brains enough to stay, we would have split $125 million. After that, every time the three of us would get together, Frank would say, 'Aren't you glad Harland talked you out of the partnership with Glen Bell? Just think, if Harland hadn't got you out of it, you'd have to hire tax consultants, accountants, and special lawyers to help you out with all that money.' It was Frank's favorite joke."

At the time of the sale, John Gorman owned 2 percent of Taco Bell's stock. Today, he continues to be active in the food industry as a consultant to restaurants and franchisees.

Taco Bell archives

Architect Robert McKay served Taco Bell as CEO from 1967 to 1981. When he started, he worked without a salary for six months. "I was convinced Taco Bell was worth the gamble, because of the uniqueness of the product in an emerging fast-food market. I trusted Glen, and he came through. We cut a deal for 15 percent of the company."

Although Bill Tilley missed out on sizable commissions from the anticipated sale to H. J. Heinz, he concedes, "Dettmer and Pearson were brilliant men of integrity, and they had done their homework."

Yet Bill himself didn't do too badly. "I was the third or fourth largest Taco Bell shareholder. I had to pay the same tax rate that Glen did, so I also benefited from a tax-free exchange instead of a taxable transaction. And to this day, I've never sold a share of Pepsi stock."

According to Robert McKay, "The fact is, it was a better deal than anyone could have imagined. Pepsi stock has gone up in value substantially each year." Robert, who in 1967 agreed to work for a struggling fast-food company without pay, a decade later was Taco Bell's second largest stockholder. He owned 10 percent, which, when the dust settled, equated to $13 million.

Robert's new wealth and Taco Bell's change of ownership made him rethink his goals. As much as he had enjoyed being the company's president, "I told Andy Pearson I didn't want to continue past three years. I had more exciting things to do than work fourteen-hour days. Also, it's hard to go from running your own business to becoming division president of a $25 billion company (which is what PepsiCo is today). You're just a little square in a management chart. They want projections, meetings, and reports. There's no time to run the business. By the time I left, I'd already made plans to open a bank and to become active in venture capital investing."

The Orange County bank Robert started in 1982, National Bank of Southern California, acquired nearly a half billion dollars in assets by the time it merged with several other Southern California banks in 1997.

At present, Robert also is chairman of the board of the McKay Foundation, a private philanthropic organization he founded "with a sizable amount of PepsiCo stock. I established the McKay Foundation to work through agencies to help people who are disadvantaged become self-sufficient and to enable them to get off welfare. It's an attempt to unify communities and minimize racial problems within California. It's tremendously rewarding."

Glen says, "McKay deserves a lot of credit for the way he handled the sale to PepsiCo. He did an outstanding job in a short time. I have no regrets and feel really fortunate. Other founders didn't do as well. The Colonel sold Kentucky Fried Chicken for $2 million. The McDonald brothers sold to Ray Kroc for $2.7 million."

Glen recalls a lunch he had with Ray Kroc during the late sixties in Los Angeles: "The day before, McDonald's stock had gone up a point, and I knew Kroc owned enough that a one-point gain earned him a million dollars. That's all I could think of when I looked at him. While he and I were sitting there, he was probably worth a million more. After the sale to Pepsi, I realized I might be in a similar position myself."

When PepsiCo acquired Taco Bell, Glen was fifty-four. At the end of January 1978, he returned to Tuolumne with resources enough to complete his dream.

Yet he felt oddly tired. "I just didn't have any fight left in me."

Marty recalls, "That was the first sign something was wrong."

Glen's Recipes for Success

#49: The best time to sell a business is when it's doing well.

In any business, you reach a point at which a transfer of ownership is best for the business, and in the best interests of the shareholders. Taco Bell had developed into a profitable, growing business with a proven track record, which made the company especially appealing to buyers.

#50: Sell to a stable, growing company you can count on to continue what you started.

When we decided to sell Taco Bell, we were in the fortunate position of having several excellent suitors. We were able to base our decision on more than who was willing to pay the highest price and offer the best terms. Taco Bell's president, Robert McKay, was an excellent negotiator. He decided PepsiCo was an ideal choice because the company would make a priority of the business we had created and help it grow to its full potential.

#51: Consider trading your ownership of your business for stock in the one that buys it.

When we exchanged stock in Taco Bell for stock in Pepsi-Co (instead of taking cash), we gained significant tax advantages. From a personal standpoint, as founder, I also received important long-term benefits. As a PepsiCo shareholder, I continued to have a vested interest in Taco Bell. I was able to reap an owner's rewards without having an owner's responsibilities.

CHAPTER SIXTEEN

Valley Center
1978-1996

IN THE FALL OF 1978, AN ANTIQUE LOGGING TRAIN pierced the blue Sierra sky with a white plume of steam. The Westside & Cherry Valley Railway, Glen's "living museum," was open to the public.

According to newspaper reports, the theme park was 5 percent complete. Over two thousand attended opening day. Glen contributed the proceeds, $8,400, to the Tuolumne Historical Society.

Though many speculated, few fully understood Glen's decision a year later not to pursue Westside's development.

Glen's former secretary, Miss Bradley, says fuel shortages during the late seventies were a contributing factor. "It was obvious that most of the people who would be attracted to Westside would come from San Francisco, but no one would go to Tuolumne if they weren't sure of getting gas for the drive home."

Moreover, the park's locomotives consumed hundreds of gallons of diesel fuel each week.

Frank Cimino, who worked at Westside with his wife Sue, says, "Mr. Bell didn't just drop it. He tried to find a good buyer who would continue to employ everyone. I think it just wasn't fun for him anymore. All the building and creativity, he enjoyed that very much. When Westside became a business, he lost interest."

Marty admits she grew tired of commuting back and forth between Sonora and San Diego. "I lived out of a suitcase. I never really unpacked."

Glen himself gives two reasons: one business, the other personal. "I was into it for about $5 million, and it was going to take $20 million to complete. If I wanted to take that chance, I needed to feel more confident. I didn't want to get caught at $10 million, and have the money in it but not the income."

Also, "Marty had a couple of close calls."

On September 25, 1978, as she waited to purchase a ticket for the 9:30 A.M. commuter flight to San Diego, Marty stood in line at the Pacific Southwest Airlines counter in San Francisco. "I could tell something was wrong. There was a pall over the airport, and the airline employees were whispering to each other." After her flight landed in San Diego, Marty learned that PSA flight 182, the one preceding hers, had collided with a small plane and crashed, killing 144 people.

"My dad came to the San Diego airport to pick me up, and as he walked past a barber shop, he saw reports of the crash on TV." One can imagine Harl Ahl's state of mind as he inquired, "Do you know what flight that was?"

Several months later, the pilot of a shuttle en route to San Francisco from Sonora told Marty the plane had lost electrical power, and the landing gear was not working properly. They would make an emergency landing.

"I wasn't frightened, because the pilot was retired from Eastern Air Lines and had years of experience," she says. "Also, I kept busy. The only other passengers were a family who spoke Spanish. I speak a little Spanish, and the pilot asked me to tell them, 'When we land, get out of the plane fast and run!' The father said they would pray, and I said that was a good idea.

"The San Francisco airport halted all other flights because of the emergency. Only one wheel of the landing gear lowered. The pilot made several passes at the ground, then touched the good wheel, the left one, onto the edge of a blacktop strip that had grass alongside it on the right. The brakes weren't working, and we cruised the whole length of the field. Then the plane tilted and one wing touched the ground. Fortunately, it didn't flip. We spun in a tight circle and stopped."

In 1979, around the time Glen sold Westside, his secretary retired. Shortly afterward, Miss Bradley became Mrs. Hill. "The two events (retirement and marriage) were not connected," she says. "But it helped that I wasn't married when I worked for Mr. Bell. There was all that moving around, and I was on call day and night. Yet I thoroughly enjoyed my job—and him. We got along, and he was forever doing things that came as a surprise." Now widowed and in her eighties, Ruth Bradley Hill—who bought Taco Bell stock during the early seventies—resides in a Florida retirement community and tours the world with a travel club she started.

The company that purchased Westside continued to operate it until 1982. According to Frank Cimino, "It was sad when it closed, but overall it was a good experience. My wife and I are better people because of it. We understand business better than we ever did before, and it was an exciting challenge away from teaching."

Glen, however, had not lost the desire to enhance undeveloped property so that others might enjoy it. "Glen is like an artist at work," says former business associate and real estate expert Bob Trujillo. "He has a huge imagination. Not too many people are creative the way he is."

Shortly after the Bells returned to Rancho Santa Fe to live full time, Glen was seduced by seven acres on La Valle Plateada. Carole Langdon, who became Glen's secretary when Miss Bradley retired, says of the property: "He had a lot of fun with it. It had beautiful topography, eucalyptus trees, and a meadow. Mr. Bell cleared the underbrush and opened up a 180-degree view. When he was done, it looked like a park, and it won an award. The Ford Motor Company used it as a backdrop for one of their brochures."

In addition, Glen remodeled a Spanish-style cottage in Rancho Santa Fe into a suite of offices for Bell Enterprises. "It was a historic house on the main street," Carole recalls. "He added fireplaces, oak paneling, and tile. Mr. Bell loves the Mexican culture, and he went to Mexico and brought back handmade chairs and a wrought-iron chandelier. People would come by for tours."

Glen longed to hunt for larger, more interesting parcels with even greater potential, but he also had pleasant obligations to family and to Taco Bell. During the 1980s and into the 1990s, Marty and Glen hosted annual reunions for his siblings, spouses, and their offspring at resorts in Utah, Idaho, California, Washington, Oregon, and Canada. Glen's older sister Deloris says, "We made sure our children did not expect Uncle Glen to foot the bill, but he usually did."

Bell family archives

1983. Bell siblings at a family reunion. Left to right: Deloris, Merrill, Maureen, Glen, Dorothy.

Glen and his brothers and sisters, though in their sixties, played like children. They threw water balloons, wore comical glasses, squirted each other with hoses, played Ping-Pong and sat on each other's laps. Deloris adds, "And when we stayed in the Fantasyland Hotel at the Edmonton Mall, Glen saw to it we had rooms with hot tubs."

Whether at hotels or in his own home, Glen also made sure his guests were well fed. According to Deloris, "Once when we stayed overnight at Glen and Marty's house, he barbecued huge steaks. And Marty was so proud of her pet chickens. For breakfast, she served us eggs from her own banty hens, in the dining room, on heavy plates."

At one gathering, Deloris and her brothers and sisters discussed their religious beliefs. "Glen was silent, just listening. Then I asked him his opinion, and he said, 'I don't know about God, but if there ever was an angel, it's Marty.' " Marty's father, Deloris adds, was "an honored guest at Bell family reunions."

Glen and Marty also visited Europe. One of their souvenirs is an advertising flier from a Taco Bell in London; it describes "Mexican Rice" as "long grain white rice cooked in a special seasoning mix with sweet corn, mild chilli [sic] sauce and a spring onion garnish." The cost: fifty-nine pence (about $1.50).

Glen observed Taco Bell's growth like a proud parent, and was an honored guest at landmark events. In 1982, at Taco Bell's twentieth anniversary celebration, he presented the Glen Bell Award to the top-selling franchisee.

A number of franchisees spoke with him. "It was a great feeling to have them walk up and say, 'Glen, remember me? I'm the motorcycle policeman who bought a Taco Bell seventeen years ago.' Or, 'Remember my grand opening in Orange County, when we both got stuck in the hot air balloon?'" The schoolteachers Glen had sold a franchise to told him they now had eight stores in Bakersfield and offered to pick him up in their private jet so he could visit.

In 1985, he sought a medical explanation for bouts of weariness and occasional hand tremors—symptoms that had developed gradually since he first felt "I didn't have any fight left in me" in 1978. Like his grandmother, Maud Johnson, Glen was diagnosed with Parkinson's disease.

Marty says, "He'd take the medication, and you'd never know anything was wrong." Even so, Parkinson's is progressive, and Glen realized his mobility would become impaired as years passed. Fortunately, the disease would not affect his mind.

"There's no cure," he says. "It's something you just accept."

During the mid- to late-eighties, while Glen spent much of his time viewing land for sale in north San Diego County, Taco Bell "mainstreamed" its image. "Adios to the old look," reported *Western Foodservice* magazine: Taco Bell's brown buildings had been painted creamy white, and store interiors had been enlarged to increase seating by 60 percent. Gone were fiberglass bells and tumbling-block letters; simplified graphics depicted a yellow bell on an orange-and-brown background. Menu boards no longer included phonetic descriptions of items—which had grown to include Nachos, Taco BellGrande, Taco Light, Taco Salad, and Mexican Pizza.

Glen became captivated by Valley Center, an inland farming community rimmed by mountains. It was similar to the San Bernardino of his youth: Citrus orchards bordered two-lane asphalt roads and flowed along the folds of distant hills; hawks soared in lazy circles; and hayfields shimmered in summer heat as though suspended in time. San Diego, with its glass-skinned skyscrapers and rush-hour traffic, was sixty minutes south.

Gary Winkelman

1996. Glen, left, and Valley Center realtor Bruce Given explore land for sale in Valley Center.

"Glen and I used to walk property all day long," recalls Bruce Given of Valley Center Realty. Bruce, who specializes in ranches, brokered Glen's purchase of four hundred acres that fronted the town's main street, Valley Center Road, at the intersection of Woods Valley Road. The former owners were an investment partnership of Hollywood stars that included Paul Newman, Tony Randall, Neil Simon, and Henry Fonda. The property sloped upward from a meadow into rocky hills, and included a stream, small lake, and a grove of twenty-five hundred olive trees whose silvery leaves formed a massive canopy.

"I have to guard against myself," Glen says. "I'll become attached to a property because of trees. I once looked at eighty acres with Douglas fir, and almost bought it because of a dozen trees, each about three feet in diameter, that grew in a tight circle. The center of the circle was like a tube. You could look straight up the middle."

Glen visited Valley Center several days a week and imagined how he might transform his Woods Valley acreage into a park. According to Glen's secretary Carole, "Mr. Bell envisioned bridges and ponds, plus an area for antique farm equipment."

Jay Enns, a contractor whom Glen hired to build storage buildings on the property, recalls, "Mr. Bell would get on the bulldozer with the operator and help him forge the road."

Few of his friends had the leisure or interest to accompany Glen to Woods Valley, and for the most part he explored its acres alone—until he met David Karle.

David, twenty-six, had plenty of time, plus the attitude that being outdoors was a privilege. A car accident five years earlier had broken his fourth cervical vertebra, and though technically a quadriplegic, David could raise his hands to shoulder-level and manipulate the joystick of an electric-powered wheelchair. For two years prior to the accident, he had been married to Barbara, a pretty blonde with light hazel eyes and a down-to-earth disposition. (Marty describes Barbara as "a drop-dead beauty.")

David says, "I told Barb, if she couldn't take it, I would understand." But Barbara never considered leaving David. They chose to live in Valley Center because it had acres of undeveloped land and country roads David could roam.

Occasionally, however, David was menaced by barking dogs. Once a cow chased him. He needed someone to "walk" with as much as Glen did, and after Bruce introduced them at a town hangout, Terry's Hay & Grain, David and Glen often set out together.

Barbara recalls, "They'd be gone for hours late in the afternoon. David would come back just stoked and tell me about Glen and his plans for Woods Valley."

David says, "He'd talk about doing a farm, nursery, and restaurant. He had the whole place planned. Glen thought of giving people horse-and-buggy tours through the olive grove. Every day it was something different. All our walks were dreams."

One afternoon, Glen expected to find David at the feed store, but he wasn't there. "My wheelchair was stuck in soft sand by the side of the road. The police went by, and when I waved, they waved back. Glen drove past, then stopped. When he got out of the car, he realized what had happened. The first thing he said was, 'Ten dollars.' I told him I'd owe it to him."

Glen and David occasionally were joined by Bob St. John, who had bought his first Taco Bell franchise with a partner in 1979. (The partnership now owns twenty-one stores.) Taco Bell had been good to Bob, and although he was aware the company's founder lived in the area, he respected Glen too much to invade his privacy.

Bob and his wife Diane were at a crowded piano bar in Rancho Santa Fe when they overheard people greet a large man who had entered as "Mr. Bell" and "Glen." Bob recalls, "My wife told me to say something to him, but I didn't have the courage, so I asked a waitress to ask if it was OK to send drinks over to his table."

Glen says he and Marty were regulars at Mille Fleurs piano bar. "We went there nearly every week for fifteen years. We didn't go there to drink—I usually ordered cranberry juice mixed with orange juice—we went to hear the piano player, Joel Nash." Joel played Big Band music and classics, and a Spanish tune Glen invariably requested: "*Malagueña.*"

"It starts out slow and builds up," Glen recalls. "We used to put our hands on the piano to feel the vibration."

With an intense dedication to business and a teasing disposition, Bob St. John doesn't seem the sort of man who gets choked up easily. Yet his emotion is evident as he continues his story: "When Mr. B and Marty came over to our table to meet us, I told him, 'Everything I have is a result of what you started. I want to thank you. The least I can do is buy you a drink.' We've been friends ever since."

Bob recalls that cattle on Glen's Woods Valley property occasionally broke through the fence. "Neighbors knew the owner was connected to Taco Bell. They'd phone me and say, 'Tell your boss to get his cattle out of the street.' I'd phone Carole, and she'd get a message to Mr. B. After he took care of it, he'd call the neighbors or stop by and apologize."

In 1987, Ed Alfaro, head of Taco Bell's "Visionary InfoWorks" department, came to Glen's office and photographed him in profile. Not long afterward, Bob and his wife escorted Glen and Marty to Taco Bell's new glass-skinned, multi-story headquarters in Irvine for the dedication of the Glen Bell Cafeteria. The photo Ed had taken was used for a bronze die-cast etching on display in the new facility.

Today, as then, visitors to Taco Bell headquarters are welcome to dine at the Glen Bell Cafeteria. It includes a sandwich deli, grill, salad bar, and hot entrees from the "Bell Bistro"—as well as standard fare from Pizza Hut, KFC, and, of course, Taco Bell. A three-hundred-seat eating area with an outside patio overlooks a massive terraced fountain. Next to the cafeteria is a gift shop that sells T-shirts, watches, mugs, and other souvenirs with colorful Taco Bell graphic designs.

Bob says, "A year after the dedication, Mr. B and I decided we wanted to see the cafeteria again. So we drove up there, parked, and went in. All of a sudden, we were surrounded by men in suits. They said, 'Bob, is there anything we can do for Mr. Bell? Would he like to go upstairs?' " Bob chuckles. "All we were doing is having lunch, but we created a mini-panic at corporate headquarters."

That same year Glen and Marty were honored guests at Taco Bell's twenty-fifth anniversary celebration in Hawaii. Among franchisees eager to meet him was one whose new store in Fairbanks, Alaska, was an outstanding success. He presented Glen with a photo of a dogsled at the drive-through window. Taco Bell's president at the time, John Martin, told eight hundred assembled franchisees that company growth had increased 186 percent over the past four years, sales had reached $1.5 billion per year, and restaurants numbered 2,700.

Glen's favorite Taco Bell was in Escondido, a city midway between Valley Center and Rancho Santa Fe. The restaurant was among those owned by Bob, whose offices occupied the back of the building. Bob says, "Mr. B likes his bean burritos and cup of beans. Three out of four times he tries to con me into paying for them."

At Bob's request, Glen would talk about Taco Bell's early days and describe his many innovations, including the way he had a fry basket modified to hold tortilla shells. When Glen said he would have liked to have invented a machine that automated the process, Bob arranged for Glen to tour one of the factories that produces tortilla shells for Taco Bell.

Bob says, "PepsiCo owns FritoLay, a company that has mastered the production and packaging of perishable corn chips. We flew to Calexico to tour the FritoLay factory in Mexicali. It was really something to see. Machines stamped out tortillas, folded them in half, and sent them down an assembly line." Production is four hundred cooked shells per minute.

At the invitation of Taco Bell president John Martin, Glen also toured Taco Bell's food research department. "They were working on breakfast

1987. Glen prizes this photo of a dog sled at the drive-through window of an Alaska Taco Bell.

Circa 1987. Glen visits Taco Bell's food research department.

items," he recalls. Proud employees explained how new methods of preparing meat and beans reduced in-store labor and provided food of consistent quality. Seasoned meat, for example, is packaged in bags designed to be heated in boiling water. Beans are dehydrated and easily reconstituted—similar to instant mashed potatoes. Menu items have become healthier: Chips are baked instead of fried, cheese is lower in fat, and vegetable oil has replaced animal fat.

Taco Bell's founder also was a San Diego celebrity. As the guest of the Padres baseball team on two occasions, Glen threw the first pitch. "You better believe I practiced it first so I wouldn't blow it."

In 1988, Glen decided to sell Woods Valley because of a moratorium on building permits within a three-thousand-acre section in the heart of Valley Center. He also sold another large parcel on Cool Valley Ranch Road north of town, and as the decade drew to a close, David saw less of him.

Also, Glen was no longer driving—"a hard thing to give up," he says. Medication for Parkinson's disease can cause drowsiness, and he had begun to experience intermittent loss of mobility in his legs and feet. "You tell your foot to move, and it won't move for you. I was worried if I told my foot to push the brake, it wouldn't respond."

1988. Glen is escorted to the pitcher's mound to throw the first pitch at a San Diego Padres baseball game.

Barbara occasionally dropped David off in Rancho Santa Fe, and the two men would walk along the golf course. But David noticed with concern that Glen's stamina seemed diminished.

In 1992, Bob St. John persuaded Glen to be Taco Bell's guest of honor at the company's thirtieth anniversary celebration in Hawaii. A limousine met Glen, Marty, Bob, and Diane at the Honolulu airport and transported them to a private jet, *Taco One*, which flew them to a resort on the island of Maui.

Glen and Marty spent time with a number of franchisees who also were friends, including Larry and Val Hahn, who had pioneered Taco Bell in Texas. Photos taken during the four-day event show Glen and Marty with Taco Bell CEO John Martin and entertainer Bill Cosby, who "did a routine that poked fun at Taco Bell," Bob recalls. Glen's sisters Deloris, Maureen, and Dorothy also attended.

One balmy evening, as the scent of gardenia rose from the hotel's gardens, Glen and Marty admired the view from the balcony of their suite. Below them, hundreds of Taco Bell franchisees had gathered for a cocktail party around the hotel pool. As the entire group sang, "Happy Birthday,

Hawaii, 1992. Glen, Marty, Taco Bell CEO John Martin.

Taco Bell," they turned, looked upward, and waved at the company's founder. "Honoring Glen was the focus of the convention," Bob says. "Mr. B was definitely overwhelmed." On the final evening, franchisees applauded nonstop during a fifteen-minute slide presentation that chronicled Taco Bell's early days. "There wasn't a dry eye in the place. A lot of people have a lot to be thankful for because of what Mr. B started."

According to a 1993 Taco Bell corporate brochure, "Glen Bell's original conception of Taco Bell has been catapulted into one of the largest fast food chains in the world. Today the Taco Bell system represents more than four thousand restaurants. Sales are nearly $4 billion annually, with more than 45 million customers a week. Employees number more than seventy thousand people nationwide."

That same year, a property foreclosure turned out to be one of the best things to happen to Glen, and possibly to David as well. Glen repossessed the 115-acre Cool Valley Ranch Road acreage, located on the outskirts of Valley Center beyond the moratorium-restricted area. Marty drove him to view it so he could assess its potential.

Hawaii, 1992. Marty with entertainer Bill Cosby at Taco Bell's thirtieth anniversary celebration.

David, who lives "within rolling distance" of Cool Valley, recalls, "If I was at my house and saw the Suburban, I'd come down. Glen wasn't doing too well. He wasn't active enough, and he needed something to focus on. I told him, 'You can spend a lot of time and money at the doctor's, which won't make you better, or you can come here. You and I are doing the same thing, just sitting around. I've got the time, if you do.' "

Glen took David's advice. By 1995, Glen had transformed the Cool Valley property into Bell Gardens, a model produce farm and landscaped park open to the public. He hired Barbara and David to run the vegetable stand and to host school field trips and garden club tours.

David says, "Creating Bell Gardens gave Glen a focus and a mission. Even after he turned seventy, people told me they had a hard time keeping up with him."

Glen's Recipes for Success

#52: Your quality of life depends on your attitude.

It's easy to get discouraged when you have a debilitating illness. With Parkinson's disease, my mind stays the same, but my body doesn't always respond the way I want it to. When simple tasks become difficult, it's tempting to just give up. I was nearly seventy when I decided not to let Parkinson's get me down any longer. I found ways to cope, and I'm proud of what I've accomplished since then.

#53: A dream is a valuable possession.

What your body can or can't do doesn't really matter if your mind works. One thing that makes people magnificent is their ability to dream. Your imagination can take you anywhere, help you envision the best of all futures, and show you how to make what seemed impossible a reality.

#54: Value people who aren't afraid to tell you the truth.

One drawback of being the boss is that employees tend to tell you what they think you want to hear. David Karle had the courage to tell me that I needed to stop feeling sorry for myself and find something productive to occupy my time. I appreciate David and others like him who say things the way they see them and do it with wisdom and concern.

CHAPTER SEVENTEEN

The Highest Bidder
July 4, 1997

"BIDDA-ONE, BIDDA-ONE, BIDDA-ONE, do I hear one-anna-quatta?" The auctioneer's rapid rhythm echoed from loudspeakers in the auditorium-sized tent.

On a platform in front of the auctioneer stood a teenage girl wearing a white shirt, white pants, and a green neckerchief—the uniform of 4-H members. She smiled at the audience as she used the curved end of a cane to nudge a restless two-hundred-pound pig. On either side of her were men called "spotters." Whenever a spotter saw a buyer raise a T-shaped bidding card, he pointed at it with a three-foot stick. Each spotter pivoted like a periscope, scanned the audience, and encouraged bids with beckoning fingers.

It was 10 A.M. on the Fourth of July 1997, and the temperature already exceeded eighty degrees. Underfoot was an inch-thick layer of damp sawdust, and its musky odor mingled with that of barnyard animals. Aisles flowed with people, many dressed in red, white, and blue for the holiday. When they spoke to each other, they shouted to be heard over the din of the auction and the roar of electric fans.

Buyers sat at rows of long tables. At one end of a middle table, his back to bleachers occupied by hundreds of onlookers, was a man in a wheelchair. Seated on his left was a woman with curly blonde hair and light hazel eyes.

Barbara Karle used the tip of an index finger to hold open an auction catalog. She pointed to the name of a Valley Center teen whose pig came next in the auction lineup, then glanced at David, who nodded.

David and Barbara started attending the annual auctions with Glen ten years ago. "Five years ago, Glen asked me to bid on his behalf," David explains. "The auction starts at 9 A.M., but we get there at 8:15 to find a table with easy access. I take a lot of pride in representing Glen, and I cherish the responsibility."

Glen and Marty, David adds, usually join them around noon. "It's pretty amazing Glen comes at all. This isn't easy for him." Difficulties include the heat, the long walk from the parking lot, and an auction that might continue past 7 P.M.

David and Glen discuss their auction strategy beforehand. "Glen tells me, 'Pace yourself. You don't want to buy too many animals right off the bat.' We set a limit of about twenty thousand dollars. But you could buy twenty pigs in one hour. At an average price per pig of three hundred dollars, that's six thousand dollars, and there are a lot more pigs, plus sheep and steers, to come. Our philosophy is to pay average and buy a lot. That way, more kids benefit. But Glen should take his own advice. At one fair I bought ten or eleven animals over a few hours, and then Glen and Marty came in and bought ten animals in a few minutes. I told him, 'Glen, you've got to pace yourself.' "

Because David has his own numbered buyer's card, he and Glen occasionally bid against each other to increase the sales price of animals that have received few bids. Yet despite their informal game plan, "Glen does things that come as a complete surprise," David says. "The auction is a lot of fun, and he enjoys a bidding war."

Only 1 percent of the eighty thousand people who swarmed San Diego County's Del Mar Fair that day came for the Junior Livestock Auction. Most fairgoers headed for the flower show, carnival, grandstand stage, or exhibit halls. Times have changed; a century ago, country fairs were farmers' gatherings, and neighbors socialized while comparing crops and livestock. The climax was the judging, followed by the awarding of ribbons and then the auctions.

A club for farm kids, 4-H began in 1912; its well-known symbol is a four-leaf clover. The organization's pledge explains its name: "I pledge my *head* to clearer thinking, my *heart* to greater loyalty, my *hands* to larger

Bell family archives

Del Mar Fair, 1975. Glen began attending 4-H livestock auctions with friend Paul Ecke, seated on his right.

service, and my *health* to better living . . . for my club, my community, my country and my world." Today, California alone has 105,000 4-H members and 30,000 adult volunteers. Members raise pigs, rabbits, goats, cattle, chickens, or sheep; or they participate in cooking, quilting, sewing, and other enrichment programs.

Glen began his support of 4-H youth in the mid-1970s, shortly after he moved to Rancho Santa Fe. "Paul Ecke, the Encinitas poinsettia grower, got me started. We met through involvement in the YMCA." Over the years, Glen has supported a half dozen youth-oriented organizations, as well as the Salvation Army, Scripps Hospital, and the American Parkinson's Association. In 1994, Glen donated a building to house a Boy's and Girl's Club unit in Valley Center.

According to Barbara, "Bell Gardens shows people over time what Glen's all about, but the Junior Livestock Auction shows a lot of people all at once."

Del Mar Fair, 1982. The Bells donate the animals they buy to the 4-H scholarship fund.

Glen says the first year he attended the auction, "I didn't know what I was doing, but I got the bidding up on the grand champion steer to eight thousand dollars. Afterward, a lot of people came and thanked me for bidding up the price, and I didn't even buy the animal. I found out later I'd been bidding against Jack-in-the-Box."

Buyers tend to be banks, corporations, grocery stores, 4-H booster groups, restaurants, and wealthy individuals, but anyone can register to bid. After their animals are auctioned, the children come and thank the buyers, and sometimes bring them small gifts.

Glen's sister Dorothy recalls, "Back in the early eighties, right after he moved to Rancho Santa Fe, Glen called and told us he'd bought an entire cow, which he'd had cut up. We were living near Long Beach, and he asked us if we wanted to drive down and get it. We hustled to rent a freezer."

Since then, Glen has donated most of the animals he has bought to the 4-H scholarship fund. "The animals go back for resale," David explains. "Money paid for them the second time helps 4-H members with college tuition."

Del Mar Fair, mid-1980s.

Glen laughs as he recalls an occasion when Barbara herself did something surprising: "The auction is a frenzied place, and things slip by you. David and I wanted to leave for a few minutes to get some exercise. There was a grand champion lamb coming up that we wanted to bid on, so we told Barbara to watch for it. If it came up while we were gone, we told her, go ahead and bid. We walked around, and I held onto the back of David's electric wheelchair. It probably looked like I was helping him, but he was really helping me. When we came back, Barbara said, 'Oh, Glen, I'm so sorry. I accidently bought you a goat.' "

Both Glen and Marty remember a ten-year-old girl who approached their table in tears. Marty says, "Her steer hadn't won a blue ribbon, and only blue ribbon animals come to auction. The ones with red ribbons have to be sold out of the barn. She asked us to go with her to the barn to look at her steer. We did, and here was this enormous thousand-pound animal. She was just this little bitty girl. She hugged the steer and kissed it and was so proud of it. She had raised it from a calf. Her mother was there, and they offered us a good price, so we bought the animal. We thought that would make the little girl happy, but when she realized she had sold her steer and had to part with it, she cried even more."

4-H kids, however, tend to be realistic about their animals. One member of a club in Valley Center wrote to Glen and Marty in June 1997: "I guess you know it's almost fair time, and I wanted to tell you about my pig. She is a purebred Yorkshire. I would really appreciate it if you would bid on my pig at the auction. It makes me sad to write this letter, but I know that my pig was raised to be a market animal. Please come and see me in the barn if I don't make it to the auction. Thank you for supporting 4-H."

Every June, the Bells receive fifty to seventy such letters from 4-H members. Barbara goes through the auction catalog and highlights each child's name, with the intent of either buying the animals or participating in the bidding so the livestock will command a higher price.

To make their pigs stand out in a crowd, kids give them clever names. Among them are: "Hamela Anderson," "Ivanna Rump," "Jerry Swinefeld," "Newt Pigrich," "Senator Fineswine," "Stan Hamphries," "Kevin Bacon," "Shaquille O'Squeel" and "AbraHam."

A high school senior wrote: "College is an expensive investment. One way I have found to help satisfy this expense is by raising swine for the Del Mar Fair. My pigs are named Tut (tuition) and Bo (board)..."

Marty says, "4-H teaches kids responsibility. They have to care for the animals twice a day, every day. They don't get a day off." She belonged to 4-H during her childhood in Indiana, and did sewing projects. Glen raised calves as a boy but did not belong to 4-H because Cedar Springs was too small to have a club.

David, Barbara, Glen, and Marty agree their most memorable experience at the fair, and also the most poignant, took place during the auction of 1995.

A chain of circumstances that led to the event began six months earlier with a tragedy that saddened the community of Valley Center. A fifteen-year-old boy, Jason Armstrong, was struck by a car as he crossed a main Valley Center thoroughfare, moments after he exited a school bus. Jason died of his injuries.

Jason's mother, Susan Armstrong, says the tight-knit community rallied around their family. "Valley Center is like an extended family. At Jason's funeral, there were nine hundred to one thousand people. That's how many lives he touched. Jason was agriculture all the way through. He loved working with animals and being on a farm." Jason belonged to both 4-H and FFA (Future Farmers of America).

Michael, Jason's father, is a large man who owns his own trucking business. At his home prior to the 1997 fair, he recalled that Jason had three jobs lined up for the summer of 1995, all having to do with agriculture. "Jason never wasted a minute."

Susan explained that six months before his death, Jason had purchased a calf with money he had earned from selling a pig. "In 1994, Jason's pig was the third highest at the fair; it went for $7.50 per pound. He paid the 'bank' (his parents), tithed 10 percent to his church, and paid five hundred dollars for a calf." At fair time, the animal weighed 1,160 pounds.

"Break-even is $1.10 to $1.25 per pound," Michael says. "Over $1.50 is a lot for a steer."

Barbara recalls, "People wondered what would happen to the steer Jason was raising to sell at the Del Mar Fair. Pretty soon, it became common knowledge that his sister Amy was going to finish the project for him. We talked to Glen about it, and he wanted to bid on the animal."

On the day of the auction, Glen and Marty had not yet arrived, but Barbara says she and David "paid particular attention" as Amy led the steer into the arena.

Both Susan and Barbara remember that time seemed to slow as Amy stood with Jason's steer at the auction block. Amy was thirteen at the time, had her mother's honey-colored hair, and the bridge of her nose was dusted with freckles. Along with her white 4-H uniform, she wore her brother's green 4-H hat; on it were two pins Jason had earned for being a member for two years.

The Armstrongs have a videotape of the auctioneer announcing, "This calf was owned by Jason Armstrong, the Valley Center boy who was killed in the school bus accident. This is his sister, Amy." As the crowd applauded, Amy turned her head to wipe her tears.

When the bidding soared past $1.50, the crowd showed its support by clapping in rhythm with the auctioneer's chant. "It was a real emotional experience for us," Susan says. "Another chapter with Jason was closing,

Courtesy of Armstrong family

Del Mar Fair, 1995. 4-H member Amy Armstrong sells her brother's steer.

and also we were watching our daughter rise to the occasion and do this for her brother."

After David lifted Glen's buyer's card at $2.65, the auctioneer shouted, "SOLD . . . to Glen and Marty Bell." Barbara says, "We felt good Glen had bought it."

The Armstrong family was thrilled, Michael adds. Not only did the steer bring an excellent price—over three thousand dollars—"to have Mr. Bell buy your animal is an honor. It's like getting a second blue ribbon."

When Glen and Marty arrived, Amy and her father came to the Bell's table with their gift, a blue baseball cap printed with the words: "I bought Jason Armstrong's steer." By then, Barbara says, "Amy was composed. I told her she had done a fabulous job."

Glen reached for Michael's hand, and the men's handshake lingered. Barbara recalls, "Tears were coming faster than Michael could wipe them away. I looked at Glen, and his eyes were full. Marty, too. David was choked up and proud. And, of course, I was crying. Losing a child, can you imagine?"

There weren't a lot of words exchanged, Michael says. "Mr. Bell knew the story. He nodded his head as if to say, 'This is a good thing.' Short and

Courtesy of Armstrong family

Del Mar Fair, 1995. David Karle with Amy Armstrong.

simple. I thanked him for buying Jason's steer and for all the support he's given Valley Center 4-H."

Michael adds, "A scripture in the Bible says, 'It is easier for a camel to pass through the eye of a needle than for a rich man to enter the kingdom of heaven.' In my book, Mr. Bell has made the grade. He shows how to have wealth but also to give."

The following March, an auction was held at Bell Gardens to raise funds to go toward construction of an agriculture-related facility at the new Valley Center High School in honor of Jason Armstrong.

Four months later, on July 4, 1997, Glen and Marty arrived at the fair at midday. Pigs were just finishing.

"The auctioneer has to go fast," Marty observed. "If they have one hundred pigs, at one minute a pig, that's over an hour and a half." Atop their table were gifts from 4-H members, including a pig-shaped pot holder and a pig-patterned throw pillow.

From the front of the tent, the auctioneer's sing-song voice continued, unceasing. A 4-H girl led a 990-pound steer, a glossy black animal with red, white, and blue ribbons around its neck, to the auction block. As she held its leather-and-chain halter, she stroked its stomach with a special "show stick" to keep it content.

"Sold one-fifty!" the auctioneer intoned, and several women seated at a table near the Bells screamed and clapped their hands.

Marty consulted her copy of the auction catalog. "Ten more steers from Valley Center. Lambs are next."

A family converged on the Bell's table, and their son, dressed in white

Del Mar Fair, 1998. 4-H member Melissa Berry of Valley Center with Glen, Kathleen, and Marty. The Bells bought Melissa's blue-ribbon lamb.

with a green necktie, posed for a photo with Glen. Next a little girl with braided hair approached him. When she extended her hand, it disappeared in his.

"Thank you for buying my pig," she said shyly. Glen nodded and smiled.

Barbara recalled with a laugh, "We once had a 4-H girl come up to Glen and ask, 'Will you bid on my lamb? I love to eat at Taco Bell.'"

When steers finished, bidding began on the grand champion lamb, which weighed 120 pounds. Glen reached for his T-shaped buyer's card, then turned to speak to David, who sat on his right. The bidding quickly escalated past ten dollars a pound; fifty-five dollars was the record.

The audience began to clap, first sporadically and then in sync with the auctioneer, who boldly increased the numbers in dollar increments. As bids rose into the twenties, and Glen and several other buyers continued to raise their cards, the crowd's exhilaration was tangible.

As he stood with his prize lamb in front of the auctioneer's podium, Justin Desimone wore the navy blue jacket and white pants of FFA members. His face was flushed, his eyes shone, and his expression blended shock with delight.

The fifteen-year-old belonged to both 4-H and FFA and lived in Bonsall, a community northwest of Valley Center. Earlier that day, Justin's eleven-year-old sister Tonina had sold a champion steer.

Glen says of Justin and Tonina, "It makes you feel good to see kids with that kind of initiative."

Justin said afterward, "When the bidding got to twenty dollars, my jaw dropped. I couldn't believe it when it kept going, past thirty, and then forty dollars."

Before each bid, Glen conferred with David. David explained later, "I've had people ask me to tell Glen what to bid, but I don't tell him what to do. I let him know where he stands and discuss strategy with him. When the bidding on Justin's lamb got past fifty dollars, I told Glen, 'You've come this far, you might as well beat the record.' "

At fifty-six dollars the crowd began pounding on the tabletops. Glen and one other bidder remained. As the auctioneer sang "fifty-seven, fifty-seven, fifty-seven, do I hear fifty-eight?" the audience turned to look at the large man in the cowboy hat, seated at the back of the room. Glen held his bidding card between the fingertips of one hand. He slowly raised it, and the crowd, which had paused to catch its breath, exhaled in a collective roar.

"Fifty-nine, fifty-nine, fifty-nine, do I hear sixty?"

Auction spotters pointed their sticks toward Glen as though they held divining rods. The mens' mouths hung open, and they didn't blink. Again, Glen lifted his card.

"It's only money," the auctioneer said with a laugh. "Sixty-one, sixty-one, sixty-one, sixty-one, do I have suh-hixty-two? Sixty-two! Sixty-two, sixty-two, sixty-two, do I have suh-hixty-three? Sixty-two, sixty-two, sixty-two, SOLD for suh-HIXty-two!"

Six hundred onlookers rose and loudly applauded the buyer who was determined to have Justin's lamb—a breeder who travels nationwide in search of the finest animals. Justin's mother said later, "I've attended the auctions for five years, and I'd never seen such a frenzy, or the way people stood and screamed."

As the audience settled into their seats, the auctioneer's voice boomed through the loudspeakers: "And let's have a round of applause for the Bell family, long-time supporters of 4-H and FFA." For the second time in fewer than five minutes, the audience honored a bidder with a standing ovation. Barbara came around to Marty and Glen's side of the table and hugged them.

A few minutes later, Justin—who had sold a home-bred lamb for a record-setting $7,440—approached Glen, shook his hand, and said, "Thank you, Mr. Bell."

Glen's Recipes for Success

#55: The greater your hands-on participation in giving, the more rewarding the experience.

At the annual Junior Livestock Auction, we enjoy meeting 4-H members, seeing the pride they take in their animals, and participating in the bidding. The auction allows us to join in the excitement while keeping a low profile. The focus of the event is not on the bidders but on the children and what they've accomplished.

#56: Support organizations that encourage initiative in children.

Everyone agrees that children are the future of America, but few give time and money to organizations that help children achieve the best possible future. Among these are the Boys and Girls Clubs, Boy (and Girl) Scouts of America, 4-H, Future Farmers of America, and the YMCA/YWCA—to name a few. I commend the Taco Bell Foundation for joining the Boys and Girls Clubs of America, in 1995, to create a five-year, $15 million program (TEENSupreme™) that promotes worthwhile activities for teens.

#57: When you accept the honor of being a role model, you also accept the responsibility.

Those of us who reaped the benefits of capitalism in the twentieth century owe a debt to the twenty-first century. Our accomplishments have changed America, and our actions continue to impact future generations. We have an obligation to honor those who came before us and to support those who follow us by upholding the principles that made America great.

CHAPTER EIGHTEEN

Bell Gardens
Autumn 1998

AT BELL GARDENS ONE OCTOBER AFTERNOON, children played tag through fields of pumpkins as big as beach balls.

Temperatures hovered near ninety, but the produce barn was cool. Its shady depths exuded the earthy scent of fresh onions and garlic.

On one wall of the barn was a crayon poster, a thank-you to Bell Gardens from the Valley Center 4-H Club. Parked outside, adjacent to the produce stand, were early twentieth-century tractors painted bright red, yellow, and green.

David Karle, Bell Gardens' events coordinator, sat nearby in the shade of a pepper tree and talked with garden club members who had come for a tour. To the east, against a backdrop of blue mountains, were acres of corn and a large lawn that flowed around oak trees, granite boulders, and flowerbeds.

David told the visitors Glen first began improving the property along Cool Valley Ranch Road in 1993. "It was full of weeds. Brush needed to be cleared and rocks moved. The wells were here, but pipes needed to be installed. We had the lawn put in, built a produce barn, and started planting crops."

David paused as a train whistle sounded beyond the cornfields. "I never thought Bell Gardens would become what it is today."

David Friend

1997. Depending on the season, Bell Gardens sells sixty-four kinds of produce.

Bell Gardens' fruit and vegetable stand opened, he told the guests, "beneath a tarp, under a pecan tree," in August 1994. "On the first day, we made forty dollars, and we were so happy. We sold watermelons and a little bit of produce. People were curious and stopped in. The stuff was so cheap that we were just making friends. Pretty soon, the idea caught on that Bell Gardens was a place to go for a picnic and to buy vegetables."

Depending on the season, the farm sells sixty-four kinds of produce. Among them are flavorful fruits and vegetables that because of a short shelf life seldom are found in supermarkets.

The farm year begins in spring with delicate, juicy strawberries grown for their exceptional sweetness. In summer, the stand's shaded bins overflow with tomatoes, sweet corn, squash, beans, peppers, cut flowers, and several varieties of gourmet melons. Most popular are fragrant Ambrosias, a luscious cantaloupe picked ripe and sold the same day.

Fall's harvest includes Indian corn, ornamental gourds, and five acres of pumpkins: minis, whites, and jack-o-lanterns, plus two popular kinds that grow to one hundred pounds or more and coincidentally have fast-food names—Big Mac and Bell Grande. Families go into the fields to pick their own pumpkins then carry them to the produce stand in green wheelbarrows.

Visitors also pose for photos alongside six-foot sunflowers, ride from the produce stand to the train depot aboard a hay wagon pulled by a vintage tractor, and tour the farm's 115 acres aboard Glen's quarter-scale train.

Glen's cowboy hat makes him easy to spot.

Afterward, they stroll through "Ghost Canyon," a walking trail amid gnarled oaks; watch adobe bricks being made from red clay soil; and attempt to navigate a one-thousand-square-foot "Corn Maize" (a maze within a cornfield).

Later that same October afternoon, a champagne-colored Lincoln passed sedately through the entry gate and turned down a dirt road flanked by rows of crayon-colored zinnias. Customers at the produce stand glimpsed in the car's passenger seat the silhouette of a large man wearing a cowboy hat.

Those visitors from Valley Center recognized Glen. They had seen him when he served as grand marshal of the town's Western Days parade, and every summer at Del Mar Fair livestock auctions.

Glen's assistant parked the Lincoln in the garage of a sprawling, single-story house used for Bell Gardens' offices, located a half mile east of the entrance on the farm's north side. It took Glen about a minute to ease himself out of the car and walk into the kitchen. On the tiled counter were tomatoes still warm from the fields. The kitchen's towels and potholders, patterned with cows and pigs, were gifts given to Glen and Marty by 4-H members.

Barbara Karle greeted Glen and told him to help himself to a butternut squash pie baked by a Bell Gardens employee who develops recipes that use the farm's produce. Beyond the kitchen was the family room, which doubles as a reception area. On the walls were framed photos from past auctions that showed dozens of Valley Center 4-H and FFA members with prize-winning animals bought by the Bells.

1994. Left to right: David Karle, farm manager Tom Edgar, Glen Bell.

Debra Lee Baldwin

1998. A miniature train depot near Lake Kathleen replicates one in the San Bernardino Mountains.

Debra Lee Baldwin

1998. Bell Gardens uses an antique White truck, similar to the one that brought Glen's family from Oregon to Cedar Springs, to display produce.

Another room was furnished only with a Ping-Pong table. Glen uses table tennis to stay limber, and he hasn't lost his touch. Visitors to the ranch house often engage him in a friendly game of Ping-Pong; one who has earned a reputation for his expertise is long-time friend Ed Hackbarth, founder of the Del Taco fast-food chain.

After two games of Ping-Pong and a slice of pie, Glen invited a guest to take a tour of Bell Gardens. Glen's preferred method of farm transportation is what he calls his "hot rod"—a deluxe golf cart modified with hand controls and a cellular phone.

Glen piloted the golf cart past acres of crumbled earth irrigated by overhead sprinklers. He paused to listen to their snik-snik-snik and watched as arcs of silver darkened the soil.

Their first stop was a small man-made lake in the farm's northeast quadrant. Wildflowers grew along the banks, reeds rimmed the water, and at one end was a rock waterfall. Railroad tracks encircled the lake, and Glen explained that a ramp across them makes it wheelchair-accessible. He tossed stale bread into the water, and soon it churned with bluegill and catfish.

A sign identified the spot as "Lake Kathleen." It's named for Glen's daughter. A miniature Victorian depot at the lake's south shore was labeled "Summit." It's modeled after the one at the top of the San Bernardino

Barbara Claypool

1998. Bell Gardens' train is an eighty-passenger model of an Electromotive GP-9, a hand-built replica of trains used worldwide during the 1950s.

Mountains where Glen hopped aboard freight trains as a teen. At the lake's north end was another sign: "Cedar Springs."

There are other hints of Glen's past at Bell Gardens. Among them are a Model A Ford, reminiscent of his first car, parked near the tractor barn; and an antique White truck, similar to the one that brought his family from Oregon to Cedar Springs, used to showcase produce for sale.

Valley Center neighbors who own llamas occasionally loan the fuzzy animals to Bell Gardens so children can see them. And in the spring, gladiolus bloom by the hundreds, a reminder of the days Glen and his siblings harvested the flowers and sold them door-to-door.

Glen next parked the golf cart in a shady area near the tracks. He described his plans for a hobo camp display, and as he spoke, he watched a green-and-yellow train with open-air passenger cars cross a trestle that bridged a creek beyond a cornfield. When the train drew near, Glen and his guest returned the waves of two dozen people riding in it.

Bell Gardens' mini-locomotive is an eighty-passenger model of an Electromotive GP-9, a hand-built replica of trains used worldwide during the 1950s. Glen purchased it from the Convair Recreation Association, retirees from the Convair Division of General Dynamics (a former San Diego

Melinda Holden

1997. Glen pounded a gold-plated spike into the tracks to symbolize the completion of the BG Farm Railway.

aerospace company) who originally built it for use in an employee park. Glen designed the layout of the train's two-mile track, which winds through the eastern half of the farm.

In March 1997, more than 350 people gathered at Bell Gardens to celebrate the completion of the BG Farm Railway. Bell Gardens employees and contractors planned the event as a surprise for Glen, who observed the festivities from the comfort of his custom rail car. Glen's yellow and green mini-trolley seats four, is electric-powered and has hand controls.

Glen received a trophy embedded with a gold-plated railway spike and a framed Congressional Resolution from Randy "Duke" Cunningham (congressman, California's Fifty-first Congressional District) that honored him as "a consummate entrepreneur and a genuine self-made American success" and praised his "vision for Bell Gardens, a pleasant country corner where families can enjoy themselves."

At the culmination of the event, Glen pounded a gold-plated spike into the tracks to symbolize the railway's completion. As onlookers applauded, a country band played "*The Wabash Cannonball.*"

Bell Gardens' train barn is a 125-foot-long garage-like structure on a knoll in the farm's southeast quadrant. Inside is a maintenance shop and space to shelter Glen's train, trolley, and several visiting locomotives. Railroad hobbyists make arrangements to run their own quarter-scale (fifteen-inch gauge) trains on the Bell Gardens tracks. The trains come to the farm in eighteen-wheel trucks.

When Glen rides his open-air train, he sits in the caboose, where he can watch the reactions of his guests as the train roars over trestles, passes areas planted with crops or flowers, or reaches a spot with an especially lovely view.

David says, "Glen gets the biggest thrill watching his ideas in action. Like the time the Model A Club came out, and all these antique cars paraded through the farm. He had so much height in his step that day. For him, all this is more than creating something beautiful. Seeing it used and watching people enjoy it—those are his real pleasures."

Glen stopped the golf cart beneath an ancient oak with bark so deeply fissured it resembled corduroy. "This is my favorite tree," he said. At first it seemed the same as countless others, but then, following Glen's gaze, his

Howard Lipin/San Diego Union-Tribune

1996. Glen traverses Bell Gardens in the comfort of a deluxe golf cart.

visitor acknowledged that overhead limbs with a zig-zag growth pattern formed an intriguing living sculpture.

Glen's sister Dorothy remembers visiting the Cool Valley Ranch property before it became Bell Gardens: "Glen asked me, 'What do you think, Dorothy? Maybe a bridge here or a bell over there?' His imagination was running wild. I couldn't believe it. The oak trees were scrubby, and they looked like trash. It's beautiful now. He could imagine how it would look."

Glen's daughter Kathleen says Bell Gardens is her father's idealized concept of "what a farm should be. It takes him back. But unlike the farm he grew up on, this one has running water, and all the equipment is in perfect working order."

Bell Gardens, Kathleen adds, "really is my dad's gift to the community. This is not a tax deduction. He does it because he enjoys giving people a place to go to. And the land is an investment."

In addition to real estate, Glen retains a sizeable amount of PepsiCo stock. When asked her family's net worth, Kathleen says with a smile, "It changes daily, depending on what the stock market is doing."

Kathleen lives in Carlsbad, a coastal community not far from Rancho Santa Fe, and is married to Steve Flynn, who works in the computer industry. She is petite compared to her father, and according to Marty, "has Grandmother Ahl's green eyes."

When Marty comes to Bell Gardens, she visits her chickens and gathers their brown eggs. The enclosure is a hundred yards from the house, and red bougainvillea grows along its screened sides.

On her way to the henhouse one Saturday earlier that fall, Marty headed first for the garage. She donned protective glasses, picked up a small shovel, and flipped the switch of a power grinder. As she sharpened the blade, sparks flew. She explained that her father, Harl Ahl (who passed away in 1995), had taught her how to use power tools.

Marty used the newly sharpened shovel to uproot a few weeds from the lawn, then opened the henhouse door and said, "Hello, girls!" A dozen Rhode Island Reds and gray-and-white Plymouth Rocks fluttered and clucked at her feet.

"Chickens are underrated by environmentalists," Marty said as hens descended on dandelion greens. "They're very useful animals and not a bit noisy unless you have a rooster. They're great little recyclers."

Despite hobbies that include gardening and playing bridge, Marty's priority, as it has been for more than forty years, is Glen. On weekday evenings, Glen's assistant takes him to one of San Diego County's many comfortable restaurants, where Marty waits for him, often accompanied by relatives or friends. After dinner, Marty drives Glen home in a GMC Suburban, a car more practical than luxurious. She has preferred sport utility vehicles for decades, long before they became popular.

Their son Gary lives in Oregon and has a son, Brandon Glen Bell, born in 1997. Gary says, "When people find out my dad founded Taco Bell, that's all they want to hear about. Sometimes I know what they're about to ask because they get a little quiver in their voice. I might joke with them and say, 'I won't tell you about my father, but I will tell you my mother is Ma Bell.' But more often I'll admit it's an amazing story and a neat thing to be close to. I'm proud of my dad and of what he accomplished."

Glen adds, "I get the same reaction from people. Neal and I were walking out of a country club in San Bernardino, and he wanted to introduce me to someone, so I shook hands with the man. Somehow Neal got around to telling him I started Taco Bell, and he said, 'No kidding. Let me shake your hand again.'"

Neal Baker, Glen's best friend since high school, recalls with amusement when they and their wives met for lunch at a restaurant on the coast, during the summer of 1997. "Glen and Marty told us they had brought us melons, corn, squash, and tomatoes from Bell Gardens. Anyone watching Glen transfer all that produce from his car into ours would have been amazed to know his net worth."

Perhaps because of his years in the Marine Corps, the compliment Glen treasures most came from retired Marine Corps commandant Lemuel Shepherd (now deceased), who was introduced to Glen several years ago by mutual friend C. J. Busick. Shepherd told Glen his civilian accomplishments have made him one of the most successful former marines.

Rex Bell, Glen's son from his first marriage, lives in Texas near his grandfather, Bernard Taylor, and has two children: Valerie (born 1974) and Chris (1982). Rex speaks of Glen with fondness and pride and describes himself, his half-brother Gary, and their father as "competitive, extremely active, and independent."

Glen's other offspring, Taco Bell, according to PepsiCo's 1996 annual report, grew 14 percent over the past five years. Stores numbered 6,890 with total sales of $4.8 billion, and per-unit sales averaged $886,000.

Glen says with a bemused smile, "We changed the eating habits of an entire nation."

In August 1997, Taco Bell president Peter Waller, escorted by franchisee Bob St. John, toured Bell Gardens and was Glen's guest for a picnic lunch on the lawn. Taco Bell's CEO later wrote Glen: "I see myself as a caretaker of the brand you created, which will be part of American life for generations to come. I'm inspired by your leadership and achievements, and consider myself privileged to lead the team at Taco Bell."

Two months later, Glen was honored at an event—broadcast to Taco Bell franchisees and employees worldwide—that celebrated the founding of Tricon Global Restaurants. The PepsiCo spin-off includes Pizza Hut, KFC, and Taco Bell. According to Bob St. John, "People lined up to shake Glen's hand. There were tears in his eyes. I knew it would get to him."

"It was a real emotional time," Glen admits. "It was hard to keep from breaking down."

In late 1997 and early 1998, Glen also attended the opening of a Taco Bell across the street from the location of his first one in Downey, as well as a franchisee convention in Hawaii.

1997. Taco Bell President Peter Waller, right, toured Bell Gardens as Glen's guest.

And on September 3, 1998, Taco Bell came to Bell Gardens to celebrate Glen's seventy-fifth birthday.

Reminiscent of an early Taco Bell grand opening, mariachis filled the air with festive music. Franchisees and old friends, including Neal Baker, Bob Trujillo, and Ed Hackbarth, toasted Glen and toured the farm. A stuffed-plush Chihuahua, representing the canine "star" of a recent popular Taco Bell ad campaign, rode with Glen in his golf cart, and a Taco Bell film crew recorded the presentation of gifts by Taco Bell corporate vice presidents.

Glen later thanked Peter Waller for a Tiffany crystal bowl that "serves as a daily reminder of a warm, ongoing relationship with Taco Bell."

Of a giant birthday card with a Chihuahua on the cover, signed by Taco Bell's Restaurant Support Team in Irvine, Glen told the CEO, "Such a

This composite photo was a gift to Glen and Marty from Glen's sister Deloris.

personal gesture of affection from your entire staff is truly overwhelming, and I am deeply grateful."

Yet Taco Bell is not the only entity that expresses the personality of a man who grew up in a verdant mountain valley, viewed trains as a ticket to adventure, and who prefers lofty trees and boulder-strewn creeks to luxury possessions.

Glen's success with Taco Bell made it possible for him to create Bell Gardens and to bring people together who help him share it with others. According to David Karle, "We're attempting to make Glen's vision a reality—to create a place where people can learn about farming, and families can enjoy themselves."

The result is a pristine, pastoral setting that brings to mind the song, "*America the Beautiful.*"

At sunset on that autumn day, the Lincoln drove past century-old oak trees, fields of melons and pumpkins, and a shuttered produce stand. As Bell Gardens' entry gate closed slowly behind Glen, tassels of corn glowed amber against distant purple mountains.

Glen's Recipes for Success

#58: Money is not a goal in itself but a means to an end.

I never saw money as something to own in its own right. It was a tool that enabled me to do other things. Start with a worthwhile dream, one that brings out the best in you and benefits others. Then use your ingenuity to pursue resources that will make that dream happen.

#59: Regardless of your circumstances, you can positively impact other people.

Being poor or in ill health doesn't mean you can't find ways to help people in need or to bring pleasure to others. However, the greater your assets, which include youth and health, the greater your power to make a positive difference in others' lives.

#60: A young man's goal should be to have no regrets when he is old.

At the end of your life, you look back and reflect on the choices you made and evaluate them according to how they helped or hurt others. Every correct decision you make now, even though it may be difficult, eventually becomes a gift to yourself.

Glen W. Bell Jr., Founder of Taco Bell

1923	*Sept. 3*—Glen William Bell Jr. born in Lynwood, CA.
1935	Bell family moved to Cedar Springs, near San Bernardino, CA.
1941	Glen graduated from San Bernardino High School.
1943	Entered Marine Corps, served in the South Pacific.
1946	Discharged from Marine Corps, returned to San Bernardino.
1947	Married Dorothy Taylor.
1948	Entered self-service food business with a hamburger drive-in in San Bernardino.
1949	*July 20*—son Rex born.
1951	Glen introduced tacos at his third stand, at the corner of Mt. Vernon and Sixth streets in San Bernardino.
1953	Divorced first wife.
1953	Opened Bell's Hamburgers in Barstow, CA.
1954	Started first self-service Mexican food restaurant, Taco-Tia, in San Bernardino.
1955	Married Martha ("Marty") Ahl.
1956	Sold his interest in Taco-Tia.
1956	*November 30*—son Gary born.

1957   Glen opened a Mexican fast-food restaurant on Colorado Boulevard in Pasadena, CA.

1958   Formed El Taco partnership with two L. A. Rams football players and Bing Crosby's son.

1960   *March 24*—daughter Kathleen born.

1961   Glen helped John Galardi start Der Wienerschnitzel in the Los Angeles suburb of Wilmington.

1962   *March 21*—Started Taco Bell chain with four-thousand-dollar investment. First Taco Bell opened in Downey, CA.

1965   Owned fifteen Taco Bells.

1965   First Taco Bell franchisee, Kermitt Bekke, opened a Taco Bell in Torrance, CA.

1966   First out-of-state Taco Bell opened in Scottsdale, AZ.

1967   *January*—Taco Bell's one hundredth store opened in Anaheim, CA.

1967   Robert McKay became Taco Bell's CEO.

1967   Summer—Glen moved to Florida to expedite Taco Bell's eastward expansion.

1967   *November*—First Taco Bell in Florida opened.

1969   Taco Bell became a publicly traded company.

1970   Glen attended MGM auction in Hollywood.

1974   Moved to Rancho Santa Fe, purchased mill property in Northern California.

1975	Resigned as chairman of the board of Taco Bell and sold stock valued at $5.85 million.
1977	Taco Bell's corporate revenues totaled $82.7 million. Stores numbered 759 in thirty-eight states.
1978	*January*—Taco Bell merged with PepsiCo. Glen acquired PepsiCo stock valued at $32 million.
1978	Westside & Cherry Valley Railway opened to the public.
1979	Glen sold Westside & Cherry Valley.
1985	Diagnosed with Parkinson's disease at age sixty-two.
1987	Taco Bell's twenty-fifth anniversary. Sales were $1.5 billion per year; restaurants numbered 2,700.
1992	Taco Bell's thirtieth anniversary celebration in Hawaii honored its founder.
1990s	Glen develops Bell Gardens, a model produce farm in Valley Center, CA.
1996	Taco Bell stores number 6,890, with total sales of $4.8 billion.
1997	Glen honored at Founder's Day, a celebration of the founding of Taco Bell's new parent company, Tricon Global Restaurants, Inc.
1998	Bell Gardens and Taco Bell celebrate Glen's seventy-fifth birthday.

INDEX